EBURY PRESS
WELCOME TO AARAAMPUR

Prof. Dhruv Nath is an angel investor, a mentor to start-ups, an author and a director with Lead Angels Network. As part of this journey, he has invested in nearly twenty start-ups, and has mentored over a hundred others. Earlier he was a professor at Management Development Institute (MDI), Gurgaon, and a senior vice president at NIIT Ltd.

He has been a consultant to the top management of Glaxo, Gillette, Nestle, Indianoil Corporation, Thermax, Bajaj Auto, Air India etc., as well as to the prime minister of Namibia and the chief minister of Delhi.

Dhruv has a BTech in electrical engineering and a PhD in computer science, both from IIT Delhi.

Welcome to Aaraampur is his debut into pure humorous short stories—and hopefully the first of many.

He would love to get your feedback either on LinkedIn or email, as follows:

LinkedIn: ww.linkedin.com/in/dhruvnathprof
Email: dhruvnathprof@gmail.com

And yes, he WILL respond 😊

Celebrating 35 Years of
Penguin Random House India

WELCOME TO
AARAAMPUR

a sleepy little hill town

DHRUV NATH

EBURY
PRESS

An imprint of Penguin Random House

EBURY PRESS

USA | Canada | UK | Ireland | Australia
New Zealand | India | South Africa | China

Ebury Press is part of the Penguin Random House group of companies
whose addresses can be found at global.penguinrandomhouse.com

Published by Penguin Random House India Pvt. Ltd
4th Floor, Capital Tower 1, MG Road,
Gurugram 122 002, Haryana, India

First published in Ebury Press by Penguin Random House India 2023

ISBN 9780143463252

Typeset in Aldine401 BT by Manipal Technologies Limited, Manipal

www.penguin.co.in

Contents

1

Let's Take You to Aaraampur

Dear reader, welcome to this book. Where I will take you to a sleepy little town, tucked away in the majestic hills of Himachal. The town is called Aaraampur. And no, that's not a spelling mistake. It's not Rampur. It *is* Aaraampur.

What did you say? You haven't been there? You haven't even heard of it? Ah, my friend, you've missed something in life. It's a truly wonderful place. If you happen to live in one of our huge, congested cities like Delhi or Mumbai or Bangalore, you must visit Aaraampur. And discover for yourself just how peaceful life in these small towns can be. No massive traffic jams, no pollution, no mad rush to get from one place to another and no desperation to save 'those two critical minutes'. Yes, you must go there. But till you visit

Aaraampur, do read this book. It'll be almost as good as the real thing.

But what if you don't have the privilege of living in one of our cities? What if you live in a small town yourself? Well then, do read the book anyway. Because in Aaraampur, you will see your own little town. You will identify with the characters, the college, the club, the events, and just about everything else I've written. And then of course, you are welcome to visit it.

So, this book is about Aaraampur. But it is also about the inhabitants of this little town. Starting with Mr P.K. Thakur, popularly known as Kaptaan Sahib. As fine a Himachali gentleman as you'll ever meet, and extremely helpful. I am told that many years ago, he had almost got into the Indian Army. Which explains why he was called Kaptaan Sahib, and not Thakur Sahib. Anyhow, after having tried out a few jobs in the city of Delhi—largely in business strategy and marketing—he happened to visit Aaraampur. One visit, and his mind was made up. Other people might have migrated to silly places like the USA or Canada, but Kaptaan Sahib was clear. He was going to migrate to Aaraampur. Along with his family, consisting of his wife (popularly known as Mrs Kaptaan, or Madam Kaptaan, or if you wanted to save your breath, simply Madam), and three children, Manju, Sanju and Panju.

But why did he decide to migrate? Simple. He had decided that he didn't want to work for a boss any more. He would pursue farming in the hills. Be his own boss, so to speak. As you might imagine, with a marketing background, he was great at convincing people, and he had managed to convince his family to shift to the small town. And so, the entire family moved bag and baggage, and set up base in Aaraampur.

But this book is not just about Kaptaan Sahib and his family. It's also about the other inhabitants of this cute little town. It's about Mangat Ram, the hard-working carpenter who always took ages to finish any project, leading his customers to tear out their hair in frustration. It's about the Pahalwaan Nai, and how he transformed himself from a champion wrestler to a barber. It's about the wonderful Dr Harish Lamba, who came to town to ply his medical trade. It's about Kaptaan Sahib's glamorous cousin who came to stay with him, and turned the male population of the town on its head. It's about so, so many of these wonderful people.

But it's not just about people. It is also about some institutions in Aaraampur. Such as the prestigious engineering college, the Popular Institute of Technology and Science, also called PITS. Where Kaptaan Sahib's two older children, Manju and Sanju, had had the good fortune to get admission. And the famous Popular Public School, or PPS for short, which the younger son, Panju, attended. And the extremely classy Aaraampur Club, which would probably put lesser-known clubs such as the Delhi Gymkhana Club to shame.

And of course, it's also about events that Aaraampur is famous for. Such as the annual wrestling championship. Perhaps even the Olympics would not get the kind of viewership that this championship did. Or the wonderful annual picnic organized by the Aaraampur Club.

But before you start reading this book (since you've bought it, I assume you do plan to read it), I wanted to share a thought. Yes, this book is about a small town in the hills. And if you live in such a town, I'm sure you will identify with Aaraampur and its proud citizens. But even if you live in a large city, just think. Isn't there a Kaptaan Sahib in your neighbourhood? Someone who takes leadership, and is always willing to help everyone? Or spare a thought for the barber who gives you a haircut. What's his story? Is it really any different from that of the Pahalwaan Nai in Aaraampur? Or the carpenter who makes the sofas for your plush drawing room in Mumbai, and keeps delaying the job? Can't you see a bit of Mangat Ram in him? Or even the college that you have been to? Isn't it remarkably similar to PITS—the engineering college that Aaraampur boasts of?

Yes my friend, human nature is the same everywhere. Whether you live in Delhi, or Chennai, or Kolkata, or our sleepy little hill town. All you need to do is dig a bit deep, and you'll find Aaraampur wherever you live.

One more thing. How do I know so much about life in the hills of Himachal? Simple—I'm from Himachal, and I've spent a large part of my life in the town of Solan, as well as Shimla. And I am as much a proud *paharhiya* as any of the other characters you will meet in the book. Yes sir, I know small towns in Himachal like the back of my hand.

Finally, after reading this book, I'm certain that you would want to visit this little town. And when you do (not if), please get in touch with me. I can actually introduce you to some of the characters that you'll be meeting in this book.

And do get in touch with me on LinkedIn at www.linkedin.com/in/dhruvnathprof, or on email at dhruvn55@gmail.com. I'd love to hear your stories. And it's just possible that your story will figure in my next book.

With that, please turn the page. Let's start with the first story. And I hope you have as much fun reading this book as I had writing it!

Bye!

Dhruv Nath

2

The Dining Table

A nd now for the first story. Where you will meet Kaptaan Sahib, who had moved bag and baggage from the busy, busy city of Delhi to the peaceful hill town of Aaraampur. But you already know all this, so let's move on.

Now, before migrating to Aaraampur, Kaptaan Sahib had made an earlier visit to the town, and had taken up a cute little house on rent. Fully furnished. The house had a sofa set, a couple of small tables, and some built-in cupboards. But the pride of place went to the dining table, with its set of four chairs. My God, that dining table was something else. It looked antique, and probably was. Kaptaan Sahib was told by the landlord that it was made of teak wood, and being the utterly gullible man that he was, he believed it. It's another matter that when his wife saw it, she immediately realized it was definitely not teak. It was probably made from cheap pine wood, which was typically used to make small crates to pack the apples that Himachal was famous for. But she didn't have the heart to tell her husband, and kept her silence. Therefore, the 'teak table' stayed on. In fact, it became the star of the household. Almost a family member, you might say.

There was only one minor issue with the table. It was just a little bit rickety. You see, it had one central leg—that's it. And this leg was not the sturdiest. Even the joint where the leg met the tabletop was not the strongest. And therefore, you can imagine the consequences. If you were to put your elbows on the table, the bowl of dal would come sliding down. Glasses of water had a peculiar habit of ending up on the floor. Rotis of course, were not an issue—you could simply pick them up from the floor, wipe off the dust, and eat them. If some of the dust remained, well, that was just too bad (in any case, the members of the Kaptaan family were fit, their intestines and various other parts of their respective digestive systems were strong; so there was no real problem). The problem was the liquids—the dal, the chicken curry, the soup. Sadly, the family was forced to cut down on their consumption of dal and curries, rather than having to clean up the floor every time.

Over the next few months, they learnt how to eat without keeping their elbows on the table, even when discussing utterly volatile subjects such as the panchayat elections in the neighbouring village of Salarghat (you see, this was a far, far more important issue than the election of the prime minister of the country, because their maid lived in this village, and the wrong top management there could be quite disastrous to the well-being of the Kaptaan family). When they did have chicken curry or dal for dinner, they had learnt that the heavy bowl needed to be kept close to the centre of the table for maximum stability. And over time, with some completely natural casualties, the family became masters at 'rickety table management'. In fact, they even took a certain quiet pride in their expertise.

But what about their friends? And their relatives, who loved to come to the hills in summertime? To understand this, let's look at a typical evening at their house:

Friend (about to place a bowl of dal close to the edge): 'Very good dal.'
Kaptaan Sahib (shrieking): 'No, don't!'
Friend (flustered): 'What happened?'
Kaptaan Madam (almost shouting): 'This table tends to shake. Please don't keep the dal there.'
Friend (completely flustered by now, drops the bowl): 'Oh no.'

I'm sure you get the idea. Over time, stories of their dining table became legendary across the length and breadth of Aaraampur. So much so, that whenever they invited friends, the standard response was, 'Why don't we meet at the club instead?' And now, dear reader, you can appreciate why the dining table had such a significant impact on the social standing of the family.

Obviously, things could not go on like this forever. And one fine day, after the nth bowl slid down and broke, Kaptaan Sahib put his foot down. 'Enough is enough,' he said. 'We're getting a new table. In any case, the amount we've spent on crockery so far, would probably have got us two tables.' Fortunately, there was consensus around the table. And so the decision was made. And written in stone. They would buy a dining table. Period.

But how? There were no great furniture shops in Aaraampur, and the closest option was perhaps Chandigarh—around eighty kilometres away. But here Kaptaan Sahib had one of his regular brainwaves. 'I know. We'll ask Mangat Ram to make it.'

'Who's Mangat Ram?' was the natural question from the family.

'A friend of mine', said Kaptaan Sahib, 'and a very good carpenter'. The second part, of course, was said with a touch of pride, as though he was personally responsible for Mangat Ram's capabilities.

Given the plethora of choices—namely one—the family agreed, and Kaptaan Sahib went off in search of Mangat Ram. He found the gentleman in his little shop, relaxing and sipping tea. Both very common occupations among paharhiyas, in case you were not aware (I should know—being a proud paharhiya myself).

'*Aao bauji. Kaise ho*?' Saying which, Mangat Ram promptly organized a second glass of tea for his visitor. After the usual half an hour of chit-chat, the topic veered around to the purpose of Kaptaan Sahib's visit, which he proceeded to explain.

'*Abhi lo bauji. Bas abhi lo,*' said Mangat Ram. Hearing which, Kaptaan Sahib's level of confidence soared, as he proceeded to explain his requirements. All through this of course, Mangat Ram kept nodding his head, saying, '*Fikar na karo bauji. Ban jayegi.*' Finally, the deal was clinched over yet another glass of tea—Kaptaan Sahib declining the very generous offer of a beedi. The time frame was fixed at one week. And Kaptaan Sahib left for home, happy in the knowledge that the family would finally have a 'dal-proof' dining table.

The week passed quickly, and Kaptaan Sahib was back in Mangat Ram's shop with a glass of tea in his hand, looking around for the table. But of course, it wasn't to be found. '*Bauji, mere jeeje ke bhatije ki shaadi thi. Par aap fikar mat karo. Bus ek hafta aur.*' And our innocent, gullible Kaptaan Sahib agreed. A glass of tea later, and he was on his way home.

The family had to go out of town for the next ten days, but they were quite excited on their return. After all, they would be seeing a brand-new table. And without wasting any time, Kaptaan Sahib went off in search of Mangat Ram and the promised table.

'*Kahaan hai* table?' he asked Mangat Ram, looking quite confused.

'*Bauji—woh dekho, maine lakdi khareed li. Bas ek hafte ki baat hai.*' Sure enough, there were a few rough planks of wood kept by the side. By now of course, Kaptaan Sahib was getting a bit frustrated. Not too frustrated, mind you, because in the hills everything proceeds at a leisurely pace, and cannot be hurried. No sir, that would go completely against the grain of any self-respecting paharhiya, and Kaptaan Sahib was, after all, a paharhiya. But a bit of frustration had definitely begun to creep in. However, that was taken care of by the next glass of tea which Mangat Ram promptly put into his hand. After extracting a solemn promise that the table would be completed by the end of the week, Kaptaan Sahib returned home. But he was thinking . . .

A week passed, and Kaptaan Sahib went back to Mangat Ram's shop. Which was shut. On being questioned, the owner of the shop next door said that Mangat Ram's wife's fourth cousin's father-in-law had passed away at the untimely age of ninety-seven. Naturally, Mangat Ram had had to go. 'Where to?' He didn't know, but apparently it was a day's journey each way.

Kaptaan Sahib was boiling when he returned home. The choicest of abuses were hurled at the little flowerpot kept in the garden since the actual recipient was not available. Of course, the poor flowerpot chose not to respond, realizing that Sahib was in a towering rage. Anyhow, having given his word to Mangat Ram, Kaptaan Sahib had no choice, so he went back a week later. And this time Mangat Ram was beaming, '*Dekho Bauji, woh lakdi plane kar ke rakkhi hai. Bas kuchh din aur.*' Not wanting to be rude, Kaptaan Sahib took the proffered glass of tea, but he was seething inside. And when he returned home his mind was made up. 'Enough is enough. We go to Chandigarh tomorrow and buy a table.'

Early next morning, the family made a visit to Chandigarh. They went into the first furniture shop they could find, and of the two ugly-looking pieces on display, selected one. That's it. They were tired and fed up, and the impact of the current table on their social standing was beginning to hurt. And therefore, the next day, Kaptaan Sahib's residence boasted of a spanking new dining table—completely 'dal proof'.

A few days later, Kaptaan Sahib happened to bump into Mangat Ram at a tea shop in the market. And boy, was Mangat Ram excited. *'Bauji, ab toh maine lakdi kaat bhi li hai. Bus kuchh hi dinon ki baat hai.'* Of course, Kaptaan Sahib gave him the bitter news. But was Mangat Ram disappointed? Come on, dear reader, you clearly do not understand *paharhi* thinking. *'Oh, aapne khareed li? Chalo koi baat nahin. Us lakdi ka palang bana doonga. Do chai laana.'* The last bit, of course, was said to the young helper in the tea shop.

And that was that. But there is more to this story, so please read on. When Kaptaan Sahib reached home that day, he was thinking. Of the time when he used to live in Delhi. The time when he had tried to get a wooden cabinet made for his home. And had tried out three different carpenters, with each being more unreliable than the others. While dealing with these gentlemen, Kaptaan Sahib had almost torn his hair out in frustration. And perhaps for the first time in this story, Kaptaan Sahib smiled. No, he was grinning from ear to ear. Yes, he had migrated from a busy, busy metro to a small, sleepy hill town. But things had not really changed. Human nature—that undefinable, completely unpredictable characteristic—was the same everywhere.

Finally, there is one last bit that I must tell you. Over the years, Kaptaan Sahib moved back to Delhi and took up a job once again. Farming was not really working out, you see. However, he loved going back to Aaraampur and reliving his days there. During one of these visits, he landed up at Mangat Ram's shop. But there he got the sad news. Mangat Ram had passed away—presumably not from overwork. His son, Duni Ram was sitting in the shop, relaxing. He asked Duni Ram whether he was a carpenter as well. Duni Ram shook his head and said, *'Nahin, hum chai ka kaam karte hain.'* Kaptaan Sahib looked around, nonplussed—there were no customers and no place to sit, except for one broken chair on which Duni Ram sat. And definitely no sign of any eatables. All it had was one kerosene stove and a couple of pots and pans. In fact, as a business establishment, it reeked of utter failure. But was Duni Ram unhappy? Of course not. He was quite content to sit on his little chair, and wait for customers to come in. If they didn't come in—well, that was just too bad.

And that, dear reader, is where Kaptaan Sahib had his first lesson in genetics. Mangat Ram might have left our world, but his genes were going strong.

In his son, of course!

3

The Business Rivalry

A few weeks after reaching Aaraampur, Kaptaan Sahib received an ultimatum from his wife, 'Either get a haircut, or become a hippy. And I refuse to be married to a hippy.' Now some people might have taken this to be a godsent opportunity, but not Kaptaan Sahib. No sir, life was comfortable, and anyway divorce was an expensive, messy affair. In any case, at his age, he was unlikely to find a new wife for himself—let alone an old one. So he gave in to the threat, and decided to get rid of his terrific, curly locks—at least partially.

The next problem was to locate an appropriate plier of the trade—in other words, a barber, or *nai*. His neighbours of course were extremely helpful. 'Go to Pahalwaan ji,' they said in one voice.

'Pahalwaan ji? A wrestler? Or maybe a body builder? What would he know about the business of cutting hair?' was Kaptaan Sahib's immediate rejoinder.

And then the story came out. You see, Pahalwaan ji was undoubtedly a professional wrestler in his younger days. And what a fine wrestler he was. His fame in pinning down opponents had spread through the length and breadth of Aaraampur, and believe it or not, even extended to nearby villages like Dadhog and Oachghat. Yes sir, our Pahalwaan ji was the toast of the town. Elders still remember the day he had pinned down an opponent from Kalaghat within just three minutes. That's it—THREE MINUTES FLAT. And this opponent had had the unpardonable audacity to challenge our Pahalwaan ji to a contest. So what if the opponent was 20 kilograms lighter than him? Such trivia did not matter to the gentry of Aaraampur. No sir, as far as Aaraampur was concerned, there couldn't be a bigger star than their very own Pahalwaan ji.

Alas, age caught up with him one day. It had to. He realized that he was beginning to lose bouts. And therefore, professional wrestling had to stop. But he had to do something to earn a living—after all, he had a wife and children to support. Fortunately, he had been a firm believer in the government's family planning programme and had limited his children to just eight. But still, this small family of his needed to be fed. Pahalwaan ji thought long and hard. For a start, he realized that he should ideally use the skills he had picked up as a wrestler, in his future profession. But where could he use those skills? Manual labour was out of the question. After all, since he had a certain standing in society. No, that wouldn't do at all. And so he continued to think . . .

. . . when one day, while sipping a glass of tea at Babu Ram's tea shop, he had a brainwave. The one skill he had definitely picked up as a champion wrestler, was the ability to grab his opponent by the hair and pull it till it hurt. In the process, some strands used to come out. And that was the answer. Why not open a hair-cutting saloon? His skills in pulling out hair would certainly come in handy. Of course, there was the small matter of a pair of scissors which was needed when the tugging didn't work, but that was okay. Pahalwaan ji was confident that he would be able to make occasional use of this fairly useless appendage.

And therefore, with a lot of fanfare, our Pahalwaan ji launched his saloon. A brightly-lit shop in the heart of town. And my, was he proud of it! He stood in the doorway as the mascot, beaming at everyone who wished to be beamed at. And did the customers come? You bet they did. They came in droves. To be honest, no one really came to him because of his capabilities as a barber. In fact, customers usually left his saloon looking more bedraggled than when they had entered. You see, you must understand the psyche of the citizens of Aaraampur. They did not come to him simply to have their hair cut. They came for the honour of having their hair cut by one of the famous sons of Aaraampur. That's why they came. And that's why they kept coming back. So life carried on, with hair in Aaraampur getting pulled and cut, alternately.

And that is how Kaptaan Sahib landed up at the hallowed portals of Pahalwaan ji. Of course, he also got a massage—but you must realize that getting a massage from an ex-wrestler is not necessarily a pleasant experience. On the whole, however, Kaptaan Sahib had to admit that it wasn't too bad. And in any case, there wasn't too much choice. Consequently, our Pahalwaan ji got one more regular customer—actually, three regular customers in the form of Kaptaan Sahib and the two junior male Kaptaans. And life carried on . . .

But as you are aware, life is rarely stagnant. It tends to throw up surprises when you least expect them. And this particular surprise came in the form of Chaman Lal's Beuty Pallor. Now Chaman Lal had just migrated from Nahan—another town in Himachal—and had set up shop in Aaraampur, just a kilometre away from our own Pahalwaan ji's outlet. Further, he had studied English for two years in school, and that gave him a significant edge over his rival. Because he had named his outlet a 'Beuty Pallor' rather than just some miserable hair-cutting saloon.

Kaptaan Sahib saw the board proudly proclaiming 'Chaman Lal's Beuty Pallor', with a bit of a shock. You see, he had grown quite fond of Pahalwaan ji by now. And in any case, he was extremely helpful by nature. It was almost as though he was personally responsible for the success of his saloon. As soon as he could, he rushed to Pahalwaan ji. '*Ab toh doosra bhi aa gaya hai*, Pahalwaan ji,' he blurted out. '*Kaun doosra?*' boomed the pahalwaan, his voice showing no signs of age. '*Woh,* Chaman Lal's

Beuty Pallor.' Hearing which, our pahalwaan barged out, leaving his current customer's face fully lathered in foam. He marched up to Chaman Lal's outlet, where his worst fears were confirmed. Yes, there *was* a Chaman Lal. And there *was* a beauty parlour. And the most terrible thing was that there was a customer sitting in Chaman Lal's chair, getting his hair trimmed. But even that was not it. This particular customer had been coming to Pahalwaan ji for the past several years, and now the miserable reptile had ditched him for this upstart called Chaman Lal. The poor customer caught Pahalwaan ji's eye, and shrank back, looking most apologetic. After all, the ex-wrestler's temper and its impact on any limbs that might get in the way, was well known. But Pahalwaan ji did not wait to see more. Breathing fire, he strode back to his saloon, and began to vent all his anger on the poor customers who had the misfortune of landing up on that particular day. By the way, reliable sources have told me that some of them landed up in the local civil hospital with minor head injuries, but this fact has neither been confirmed nor denied till date.

Anyhow, Chaman Lal's smart branding strategy worked and the curious male population of Aaraampur started trickling in. 'Beuty Pallor? *Chalo* try *karte hain*,' was the general refrain. Now Chaman Lal was good—at least when compared to the other local practitioner of the trade. Further, he did not have a background in wrestling, and therefore his use of the scissors was far more frequent than that of Pahalwaan ji. And therefore, his business continued unabated.

Now you can imagine the impact this intrusion had on our very own Kaptaan Sahib. You see, this gentleman had almost adopted Pahalwaan ji by now. His success was Kaptaan Sahib's success, and his failure was Kaptaan Sahib's failure. In Kaptaan Sahib's mind, any miserable wretch of a competitor, who anyway had no business to be in the little town of Aaraampur, had to be handled with an iron fist. This was almost like the rivalry between Amazon and Flipkart. Or between Reliance Jio and Airtel. And Kaptaan Sahib was quite determined to ensure that in this war, Pahalwaan ji's business came out trumps.

All his skills in marketing came to the fore as he advised and guided Pahalwaan ji. The starting point, as you might imagine, was a rebranding of the saloon. I'm not sure what the new brand was, but I do know that next to the name on the board of the shop, there was a picture of the massive Pahalwaan ji. Beaming away, with a pair of scissors in his hand, standing next to a puny customer. Just in case people didn't realize that this was a hair-cutting saloon. And then of course, the entire shop was repainted. There was a major tussle between Pahalwaan ji and his mentor on the colour of the walls. Kaptaan Sahib would have liked soft off-white walls, but Pahalwaan ji would have none of it. No sir, the walls had to be painted a bilious green. With the inevitable photographs of film stars adorning them.

Then of course, there had to be a WhatsApp campaign, which is so essential in modern business warfare. And finally, the 'pièce de résistance'. Something that Kaptaan Sahib was inordinately proud of. An absolute master

stroke, if there was any. The package deal. 'Come for a
haircut and get a shave free!'

Yes sir, Kaptaan Sahib and his protégé tried all the
tricks in the trade. And some more that had not been tried
earlier. But do you think they worked? Come on, don't be
silly. If they had worked, wouldn't my story have ended
right here? That's right. Nothing worked, and Pahalwaan
ji's business saw a steady decline.

On a different note, there is something else you need
to be aware of. The relationship that developed between
Chaman Lal and Pahalwaan ji. None! That's right, there
was no relationship. When they passed each other on
the road, Pahalwaan ji would suddenly develop a keen
interest in his massive chappals. And Chaman Lal would
simply look the other way. I'm sure you have seen social
graces in small towns, where everyone knows everyone
else, and throats go hoarse through wishing each other,
'Ram Ram ji' all day long. But no, there was simply stony
silence when these two masters of tonsorial skills met.
And by the way, the relationship between Pahalwaan ji's
mentor, namely Kaptaan Sahib, and Chaman Lal, was not
much better. That was the kind of person Kaptaan Sahib
was. He would stick by his friends through thick and thin.

All through this, our Pahalwaan ji kept brainwashing
his customers against the 'Beuty Pallor'. *'Arrey, wahaan jaoge
to ganje ho jaoge. Phir mujhe kuchh mat bolna,'* he would say,
with a vicious tug at the hair of whichever poor customer
happened to be in his chair at that moment. And then
the parting shot, *'Jaana hai toh jao.'* You see, Pahalwaan ji
had many wonderful qualities, but subtlety was definitely

not one of them. Of course, the helpless customer had no option but to agree. After all, no one wanted to disagree with Pahalwaan ji, when his massive hands were all over his cranium.

One fine day however, there was a twist in the tale. Because on that fateful day, Chaman Lal's nephew happened to walk into Pahalwaan ji's saloon.

Our pahalwaan almost exploded.

'*TU? TU YAHAAN KYA KAR RAHAA HAI?*'

When he had stopped quaking in his shoes, the poor young boy replied, '*Chacha ji ne aapke paas bheja hai.*'

'*KYON?*' thundered the wrestler.

'*Unhone dukaan bandh kar di hai.*'

'*Bandh kar di?*' said Pahalwaan ji, in a somewhat milder tone, if that were possible. And slowly, ever so slowly, the story came out. Apparently Chaman Lal's father in-law had convinced him to shut down the Beuty Pallor and set up a dhaba instead. He believed that that was more in keeping with the exalted social standing of the family. Chaman Lal did object, but the carrot of full funding for the new venture was simply too much to resist. And so, the Beuty Pallor closed down, and a spanking new Chaman's Shudh Baij Dhaba came up in its place. With the name making it abundantly clear that meat was not served there.

There was a smile on the Pahalwaan's face as he gently caressed the young nephew's hair. Wonder of wonders, he also forgot to tug at his hair, as the scissors did their job, snipping away happily. And that evening, when the two erstwhile business rivals met, they did not ignore each other. No sir, they said, 'Ram Ram ji,' with enthusiasm. Because the pahalwaan had taken his entire brood—his wife and eight children—to have dinner at Chaman Lal's dhaba. Along with his mentor, Kaptaan Sahib, of course.

That's right. Lesser business empires like Airtel and Jio might still continue to fight it out. And so, for that matter, might Zomato and Swiggy. But a far bigger business rivalry, which could have shaken the very foundations of Aaraampur, was at a happy end.

4

Romance Comes to Aaraampur

No book can be complete without its share of romance. So how can this book be any different? That's right, I'm now going to tell you about the time when half the adult male population of Aaraampur was galvanized into action. Yes sir, that was the time when our sleepy little town had its first whiff of true romance. . .

It all started soon after the Kaptaans moved to Aaraampur, when Kaptaan Sahib's cousin came to stay with them.

Ah. His cousin. A breath of fresh air, if ever there was one. You could say that glamour had finally come to Aaraampur. Forty-something in age, Ms Thakur appeared to be unmarried. Rumour had it that she was divorced—but no one actually had the courage to ask, and

the Kaptaans were not about to divulge this information.
So the rumour stayed.

However, that is not the point. You must understand
the impact that Ms Thakur had on the population of the
town. Specifically on the adult male population. Suits,
ties and pocket squares suddenly came out of the closet.
And the local dry cleaner had a field day, sprucing up his
clients. But to discuss this in detail, we need to divide the
population along demographic lines, as follows:

First, there were the married men. The ones who
cursed their luck and regretted the day they had got
married (as you might imagine, this thought used to
come up regularly, but this time it was the real thing).
Divorce, of course, was out of the question. Such things
only happened in Delhi or Mumbai. They simply didn't
happen in decent households in Aaraampur. So they
had to be satisfied with cursing their luck, and smiling
at the lady in question whenever the opportunity came
their way. And hoping that her cousin would invite them
home. In any case, their wives were smart and kept a
hawk's eye on them—even when they went out shopping
for *gobhi* and *aaloo*.

Next, we had the oldies. The seventy- or eighty-
somethings. Those who were quite happy to talk to this
lady. So what if she called them 'uncle'? The important
thing is that she called them. These oldies had figured
out that Ms Thakur had a reasonably regular schedule.
For instance, there was a specific time when she went out
for a walk. And by sheer coincidence, they happened to

be around when she walked by, just to hear her call out, 'Hello uncle.'

But the men I really wanted to talk about here, were the confirmed bachelors. Aged between sixty and seventy, although there were a couple of candidates above seventy. These were men who had staunchly refused the option of marriage, and were leading the life of a free bird, unencumbered with stupid things such as schooling, colleging, parenting, and above all, constant nagging. They would spend their time at the Aaraampur club, have their drink (or rather drinks), and generally led contented lives. Until now. Because now Ms Thakur had arrived on the scene.

But hang on. As usual, I'm getting ahead of myself, so let's get specific. While there were a few dozen potential applicants for the hand of Ms Thakur, the serious competitors boiled down to just three. First of all, there was the psychiatrist, Dr Sood. Now you might ask what a psychiatrist was doing in the little town of Aaraampur? Frankly, I don't know. There was a rumour that he had been practising in Delhi, but most of his patients had ultimately ended up in a mental asylum. And therefore, he had shifted to Aaraampur to start afresh, with a brand-new set of patients. I'm not too sure whether the rumour was based on facts, but anyhow, that's not too relevant to our story, so we'll let it pass. To get back to the gentleman, he was sixty-five, but a very well-preserved sixty-five. In fact, he took immense pride in the fact that he didn't look a day more than sixty-four and a half. Unfortunately, he had a terrible squint, which had an almost mesmerizing

effect on whichever patient was on his couch. Once again
however, this has no relevance to this story.

Then there was Mr Bhagat, all of sixty-three years,
and perhaps one of the biggest landowners in Aaraampur.
I'm not sure he was actually the biggest, because I never
really had the opportunity to measure the size of his land
holding and compare it with that of Mr Roop Singh and
Mr Bajaj, the two real estate barons of Aaraampur. But
even if it wasn't, it certainly ran the others very, very
close. Bhagat ji took immense pride in his property. So
what if it was entirely inherited from his father, and he
himself had done nothing to add to it. In fact, he had
subtracted from it. You see, Bhagat ji was a bit averse to
work. He had never done an honest day's work in his life.
Perhaps not even a dishonest day's work. Now as you are
aware, every human being needs just a *leetle* bit of money
for food and drink—largely drink. And what better than
to sell off pieces of the inherited property from time to
time? Smart, wasn't it?

And then, of course, there was the dapper sixty-eight-
year-old Mr Kochhar, the owner of Kochhar Stores,
the largest store in Aaraampur. You might say it was the
Walmart of Aaraampur. Kochhar Sahib was the talk of the
town for his business acumen, and the consequent success
he had achieved. And for the fact that he was always
impeccably dressed—a three-piece suit even when it was
boiling in summer, complete with a cravat, a stylish hat,
and of course the inevitable walking stick. Every morning
used to see Mr Kochhar standing at the entrance to his
shop, with his chest puffed out ever so slightly, trying to

appear nonchalant. But of course, the admiring glances of
the townsfolk said otherwise. Yes sir, Kochhar Sahib was
the talk of at least the male population of the town, and not
just because he had had the good sense to not get married.

And now that you've met these gentlemen individually,
let's meet them together. These three were the best of
friends. Every evening, you could see them in the club,
each with a drink in his hand. They would play cards,
enjoy a smoke, and do whatever else you do in a club. In
the several years I lived in Aaraampur, I have never seen a
day when they did not have their evening rendezvous in
the club. Now don't get me wrong—this does not mean
that I spent most of my evenings there. I just happened to
know the *chowkidar* of the club, and he had once told me
this in strict confidence.

But all this was shattered the day Ms Thakur appeared
on the scene. As I have mentioned, on that day the male
population of Aaraampur went through a minor upheaval.
But that's not really of interest to us. What is of interest
is what happened to our three friends. Starting with Mr
Kochhar of Kochhar Stores, who was standing in the
doorway of his shop as usual, that fateful morning. And
then he saw the vision. And almost gaped. Of course,
he recovered quickly and doffed his hat to her, as any
gentleman would. And she responded as any lady would,
smiling vaguely in his direction. Now you can imagine
what poor Kochhar Sahib went through. That's right,
he was well and truly smitten. All his bluster about not
marrying was gone. The rest of his day passed in a bit
of a daze, with most of his customers quite surprised at

the ridiculously low prices of items in his store. They thought it was a clearance sale, but of course you and I know better, don't we 😊?

And then we come to Dr Sood. When he saw Ms Thakur, his reaction was not too different from that of Mr Kochhar. Except that he had no hat to doff. But in his confusion, his squint became more pronounced, leading the lady to look at him sympathetically, '*Poor old man. What a terrible squint he has.*' That sympathetic look completed the picture, and Dr Sood promptly joined the likes of Mr Kochhar. Yes sir, he had become a devotee as well. For the next few days, Dr Sood had a permanently dreamy look in his eyes. With disastrous consequences for his patients, as you can imagine!

Finally, what about Bhagat ji? This venerable gentleman saw Ms Thakur in the market, while he was buying a *kaddu*. Quite naturally, he dropped the kaddu, and had to pay for the remnants even though they were inedible by now. But what followed was more important. Completely floored by now, Mr Bhagat proceeded to buy a total of eight kilos of vegetables from this shop. He wasn't even aware of what he was buying. Dreamily, he carried the burden home, and handed it over to his faithful cook, saying '*Aaj* dinner *mein sab kuchh bana do.*' Leading the cook to whisper to the family cat, '*Sahib paagal ho gaye hain.*'

So that's what happened to our three fast friends during their first meeting. But we now need to look at what happened next. Actually, three specific things happened. First of all, Kaptaan Sahib became surprisingly popular. Each time one of these three suitors met him on the street, they would stop and chat with him and ask him if there were any problems he was facing, being new to the town. And then they would land up at his house to ask the same question, in the hope of meeting Ms Thakur. They also invited him to their respective homes—with family of course. Unfortunately, while Kaptaan Sahib was delighted to accept their hospitality, the family—specifically one member of the family—never came along. But that, of course, never deterred our good Kaptaan Sahib from repeatedly commenting, 'What amazingly warm and friendly people we have in this town.'

What's the second thing that happened? Well, for this, I need to share a bit of information with you. You see, Ms Thakur had a pet dog—or doggie, since it was rather small in size. And she wouldn't go anywhere without it. You can now guess the strategy adopted by our three venerable bachelors. That's right, they decided to focus on the doggie. 'Lovely doggie', 'cute doggie', 'doggie wants a biscuit,' were some of the terms that were thrown around when the doggie appeared on the scene along with its mistress. And they would continuously pet the little doggie. The fact that all three of them were dog haters had nothing to do with it. Incidentally, the doggie hated them as well, and made its views amply clear by barking at them and snapping at their heels. While its mistress wished the old men would go away and let her continue on her way.

But the most important thing that happened is yet to be told. What I am about to say now has to do with the friendship between these three hardened bachelors. You see, each one of them realized that the other two were competitors for the hand of the fair maiden in question. Now, I'm sure you've heard the old saying, 'All's fair in love and war.' And this was not love. It was out-and-out war. These friends of several decades simply stopped talking to each other. When they met on the road, they studiously avoided looking at each other. Wonder of wonders, they even stopped having their regular drink every evening. No that's not strictly correct—I meant that they stopped having a drink *together*. They would still go to the club, but they would sit at separate tables, nursing their respective drinks. Glaring at their competitors from time to time. The bartender later told me that the quantum of alcohol consumed by these three had actually tripled during this period.

And so life carried on . . .

But somewhere, something had to give. And one fine day, it did. Because Ms Thakur's fourth and current husband landed up in town.

Did you hear right? Did I say fourth husband? That's correct. This was her fourth husband, picked up after three successful divorces. And this one was not divorced—they were only separated. Legally, they were still married. Anyhow, this gentleman appeared on the scene and whisked his wife away to Bangalore.

There was stunned silence in our little town. And then the tongues began to wag. 'Fourth husband? I knew it.' Or 'My God, what a woman'. Or even, 'Good riddance. We don't want people like this around town. Bad influence on our men'. The last bit, of course, was said by the married ladies in town, with a collective sigh of relief.

Now, I'm sure you are wondering what happened to our three suitors? Well, after the initial shock, they began to console themselves. 'She was not the right person for me anyway.' Or 'Thank God. I escaped just in time'. Or a more positive, 'I'm sure there are better things around for a highly eligible person like me'. As you can see, our friends had accepted reality. Perhaps learning from Aesop's famous fable, *The Fox and the Grapes*. Most important however, now that the prize they were competing for, had been cruelly snatched away from their grasp, our three rivals became friends again. And started their regular visits to the club as before. Sitting at a common table and thanking their lucky stars that they had had the sense to remain bachelors. Of course, their visits to the Kaptaan household also came to a grinding halt. Yes sir, our three rivals were back to their confirmed bachelorhood.

And our sleepy little town went back to being a sleepy little town.

But before I end this story, there is one thing I must tell you. Something that relates to our good old Kaptaan Sahib. Till today, he has not been able to figure out what had happened to the amazingly warm and friendly people of Aaraampur.

Of course, I didn't have the heart to tell him.

5

The Engineering College

Dear reader, while reading this book you might have got the impression that the only thing Aaraampur boasted of was carpenters, barbers, *halwais,* tea-shop owners and the like. Nothing could be further from the truth. The town also had its famous institutions. Starting with that one institute of higher learning that every Aaraampurian (citizen of Aaraampur, in case you hadn't got it) was inordinately proud of. Their engineering college. My God, this college was something else. Located on the outskirts of the town, the college was the veritable seat of all learning. From computer science to electrical engineering, to mechanical engineering, to . . . it taught everything you could think of. And more. Complete with two state-of-the-art hostels—one for boys and the other for girls. You see, bad practices such as co-ed hostels, which are so prevalent in the world today, had not yet touched our sleepy town of Aaraampur. By the way, I am told this college ranked a staggering eighteenth in the district. Yes, you heard me right—*eighteenth in the entire district*. Wasn't that something to be truly proud of?

What was the name of the college? Well, since you asked, it was called the Popular Institute of Technology and Science, or PITS for short. I'm sure you've heard the name. And given its exalted status, the wonderful folks of Aaraampur often called it '*The* PITS'.

And now for the best part. Kaptaan Sahib's daughter, Manju, had just secured admission to this college and had joined a month ago.

Ah! What an achievement. To gain entrance to these hallowed portals of higher learning, was a dream come true. Not only for Manju, but for her entire family. Her parents were overjoyed. Phone calls and WhatsApp messages went out to *mamas* and *chachas* and cousins across the length and breadth of the country. And of course, everyone was equally excited. After all, no one in the family had ever got admission to such a prestigious institute!

So much for the background. And now for our story. Manju joined college and was a good, conscientious student—the kind that attended classes, took copious notes, and did well in her exams. A kind of model student, if you get what I mean. She stayed on campus, as was the rule, and came home over weekends. However, on one particular weekend, she didn't come home. Instead, she called up Kaptaan Sahib. And in her excitement, she was literally eating up her words. You see, Manju had always

been keen to do something for society, specifically for
its less privileged members. A few months ago, she had
actually given one rupee out of her hard-earned pocket
money to a beggar. And was she proud of it? The look
of supreme gratitude on the beggar's face made her
realize that she was destined for far bigger things. It's
quite another matter that the look on the beggar's face
was one of utter disgust, not gratitude! One rupee! What
rot! Even beggars had self-respect, after all. Anyhow, our
young friend Manju was now convinced that she had a
major role to play in the upliftment of her fellow human
beings. And once she landed up at PITS, she heard of the
Social Work Society—or SWS—which did exactly that.
They would collect and distribute warm clothes to the
poor, they would take tuitions for young children who
could not afford them, and they would feed the poor on
festivals. But what Manju liked most was the fact that they
had adopted a village named Baisal, a few kilometres from
campus. Where they would land up from time to time and
carry out development activities. Manju couldn't believe
her good fortune. This is what she had always wanted to
do. In a jiffy, she signed up and became a proud member
of the Society.

Kaptaan Sahib was equally delighted. He had also
been involved in similar activities when he was in college
in Delhi, and was very happy that his daughter was
following in his footsteps.

Finally, the big day arrived. The day the SWS was
to make its monthly visit to Baisal, to continue the
good work they had been doing for years. And now

dear reader, you can understand Manju's excitement. Because she—yes she, Manju—would be going along to Baisal as part of the SWS, and would help develop the village. She thought of the grateful villagers in Baisal, and a beatific smile came over her face. You see, Manju was a true dreamer. She imagined that the villagers would fall over themselves to thank her once they saw the work she and her colleagues had done. And of course, she would accept their thanks in all modesty. And agree to be an honoured guest of the sarpanch whenever she visited the village. And politely refuse the hand of his elder son. And . . .

Unfortunately, she had to come back to earth, because the bus that was to take them to Baisal was about to leave. Today they were supposed to dig a canal to help the villagers irrigate their fields. And since this was a premier engineering college, the planning was meticulous. Everything had been chalked out to the minutest of details, all the way from the shovels, pickaxes and whatever else they needed to dig the canal, to the carefully packed, semi-cooked *paranthas* that the hostel mess was renowned for. With everyone on board, the bus started, with the students singing all the way—after all, it was a good deed they were going for.

Once they arrived in Baisal, the leader of the gang—a second yearite—told them where the canal was to be dug. And with shovels in hand, our young budding engineers got down to digging in right earnest. It was hard work, the soil was rocky, but the students were quite determined. And the work progressed steadily.

Interestingly, they were not alone. A curious group of villagers—smoking the occasional *beedi*—stood nearby and watched them hard at work. Of course, our students understood. These were the grateful villagers who were just waiting for the canal to be dug. Anyhow, the work went on, till finally they called a halt for lunch. After all, these youngsters were not really used to physical work of this kind, and they were, quite naturally, tired. They put away their shovels and tucked into the shapeless and tasteless *paranthas*. So what if they were half-cooked? The youngsters were hungry, and the meal was demolished in no time.

Lunch over, they took a short break, and then got back to work. Once again, the villagers stood nearby with inscrutable expressions, and watched them. However, a close observer would have noticed that their numbers were larger than before, and some of them had frowns on their faces. Anyhow, this was irrelevant to our busy, busy workers, who carried on manfully. Till at last the canal was complete. Standing back, they surveyed their handiwork with pride. How useful the canal would be for the villagers. Finally, they would be able to irrigate their fields. And with this thought, our young PITSians said namaste to the villagers, and climbed back into the bus. Yes, they were a tired lot, but they were extremely happy. They reached the PITS campus, had a quick dinner, and went to their rooms to bed. Including our friend Manju, who was fast asleep in minutes. And it was the kind of sleep that comes to happy people—those who have done great work. She dreamt that the villagers came to visit her and were touching her feet. And then the chief minister of Himachal called Manju to his secretariat, and was asking her to supervise the digging of canals across the entire state. Suddenly, there was a phone call from the prime minister, asking for her advice on the interlinking of all rivers across the country. The dream became more and more real . . .

Till suddenly, the prime minister threw a glass of cold water in her face. Surprised, Manju opened her eyes and saw her roommate with an empty mug in her hand, 'Class *nahin jaana hai?*' Of course, Manju was new to PITS and hadn't yet got into these delectable habits, so she rushed to change (brushing her teeth was out of the question—it was late, and this particular professor never gave attendance to latecomers). And so the Baisal project was forgotten for the moment.

Yes, Manju had forgotten Baisal for the moment. But we cannot. We must go back and see what was happening the day after this major infrastructure project was completed. Because the villagers had got together and were filling up the canal once again.

That's right—you heard me right—they were actually filling up the canal, which had been dug with such love and affection the previous day.

But why on earth . . .?

Because our young PITSians had dug the canal at the wrong place. The planning had been meticulous, and the execution as perfect as it could be. But the location had gone horribly wrong. And therefore, whatever they had done was being undone by the villagers.

Anyhow, let's get back to PITS. A day after this visit, Manju happened to meet her senior, BN. Incidentally, BN had been part of the SWS the previous year but had now left for reasons that I don't know. 'How was it?' asked BN. 'Great,' replied our young friend Manju. 'We dug a canal which they really needed for their irrigation.' Saying which she beamed at BN. Surprisingly however, BN wasn't impressed. She simply smiled in a strange sort of way, and asked, 'When is your next visit to Baisal?'

'Sometime next month,' said Manju, and you could sense the excitement in her voice.

At the same time, she was a little surprised by BN's lack of enthusiasm. After all, they had done great work— at the very least she should have complimented Manju.

A month later, the next visit to Baisal was scheduled. This time, the students had to construct a wall. A very important wall, since it would keep stray animals away from the grain that had been harvested. Once again, the youngsters picked up their tools (trowels this time) along with the bags of cement required. Bricks of course would be made available on the spot—after all, the villagers had to do *something*. They couldn't bank on PITS for everything, could they?

Once they reached Baisal, the first thing Manju did was to check on the status of the canal they had dug a month earlier. She was just itching to see it bringing water to the fields. She reached the spot where they had dug the canal.

And stopped.

Where was the canal? She was sure of the spot—there were two huge *peepal* trees near it, and she couldn't possibly mistake the location. But there was no canal to be found. Instead, there seemed to be a new canal around fifty feet away. Perplexed, Manju decided to drop the matter. Maybe she was mistaken. Yes, that was it—she had been quite tired that day, and she must have been mistaken. Mystery solved, she bent to the task of building the wall, along with the others.

The students worked all day, and at the end of it, stepped back to survey their handiwork proudly. It was truly an engineering marvel—just the thing that PITSians were capable of. Once again, a quick namaste, and the gang returned to PITS.

That night, Manju's dream was different. She dreamt that she was the CEO of a large real estate company and was just embarking on a large housing project. But just as she was about to start, she got an urgent call from the Ministry of Housing, pleading with her to take up the construction of one lakh houses for the poor. They were desperate to have her, since no one else had the capability to build these houses. Manju was now torn between these two assignments and couldn't figure out which one to take up. Till of course the Minister for Housing picked up a loud, raucous sounding bell, and held it close to her ear. Manju woke up and realized it was the alarm on her phone, reminding her to get up and reach her class.

And what about Baisal? Well, the villagers had checked the wall and found it too weak to last. You can, of course, imagine the rest. The wall was promptly demolished by the villagers and constructed again. And this time, a close observer would have noticed that most of them were looking angry. In fact, some of them were grumbling openly.

In the evening, they landed up at the house of the sarpanch. '*Sarpanch ji, yeh* students *sara kaam bigaad dete hain. Pehle galat jagah neher khodi. Aur is baar kacchi deewaar bana di. Har baar hamara kaam badh jaata hai.*'

The sarpanch took a deep draught of his hookah, but said nothing.

And then one of the villagers continued, '*Naak mein dum kar diya hai inhone. Chhodte hi nahin hain. Aap kyon inhein baar baar bulate ho?*'

That is when the wise, old sarpanch spoke, '*Arrey bhai, in* students *ko seekhna hai na? Humare yahan nahin, toh ingineering kahaan seekhenge?*'

Saying which he took another deep swig of his hookah.

And then he continued, '*Dekho bhaiyon, hamein bhi toh desh ki bhalai ke baare mein sochna hai. Hamare yahaan se yeh* student *log seekh ke jayenge, toh bade ingineer banenge. Desh ka kitna bhalaa hoga, na?*'

The rest of the villagers pondered over these wise words. And finally nodded. As usual, the sarpanch was right. The village was doing major work for society. They were training students from one of the best engineering colleges in the country. They were actually doing significant social work. And with this thought, their chests swelled up with pride, as they inhaled deeply on their respective *beedies*.

There is of course a footnote to this story. By now the SWS at PITS decided that they had done enough social work in Baisal, and the villagers could now manage on their own. Therefore, they adopted a fresh new village named Sadhughat for their largesse. Baisal was now done and dusted. But the members of the SWS, including our friend Manju, were truly happy that they had done so much for society.

And of course, the villagers at Baisal were equally happy that they were doing great work by training budding *ingineers* at PITS.

In short, everyone believed they were doing great social work. And everyone was happy. . .

6

The Picnic

I'm sure you have heard about the Aaraampur club. If you haven't, you've missed something significant in life. A visit through its hallowed portals is like a visit to the famous pyramids of Egypt. Or even seeing the Eiffel Tower all lit up at night (not in the daytime— that's commonplace). Closer home, being invited to the Aaraampur club is like being invited to Rashtrapati Bhavan. And of course, its members consider it to be at least a couple of notches above the Delhi Gymkhana club in the pecking order. At least, that's what the good citizens of Aaraampur would have us believe.

As you might expect, Kaptaan Sahib was a member. Not just a member, but a very important member. Any activity in the club, and you could be sure that he was involved. And therefore, when the club had its annual picnic, Kaptaan Sahib was the chief organizer.

Now, I must tell you something more about this picnic. The club would take you to exotic locations like Dochi or Subathu, or even the majestic hills of Jubbal. Everything was organized by the club, starting with the food and ending with the transport in the form of a van. The members needed to pay for the picnic, of course, but after that their worries were over. And our story begins with one such picnic, which took place in the scenic village of Manerghat.

On that auspicious day, the members who were part of that hallowed trip landed up at the club in all their finery. Ladies appropriately decked up in their finest gold and diamonds, and the men looking quite dapper in their *bandhgalas*. After all, this was no ordinary picnic. It was a veritable fashion show. With each person looking at the others with a smirk, as if to say, 'How overdressed he (or she) is. What vanity!'

At the centre of it all was our very own master of ceremonies, Kaptaan Sahib. Bustling around, looking terribly busy (I suspect he wasn't too busy, but then it wouldn't do any harm to look busy, would it?),

The van was ready, along with its smiling driver, Hukam Singh. After the members climbed in and took their seats, off it went. The hills were a vivid shade of green—quite at their post-monsoon best—and the drive was lovely. A couple of hours later, the party arrived at Manerghat and walked to the picnic site, which was a cute, hooded glen, a few hundred metres beyond. And what fun they had all day. There was music and dancing and tambola and cards, and everything else a wonderful picnic should have. They also had musical chairs—minus the chairs of course. On the menu were *poories* and *parathas* and *biryani* and just about anything you can imagine—except crabs. It was such fun.

However, all good things must come to an end, and so did this picnic. Late in the afternoon, the happy citizens of Aaraampur decided to wind up. Having gathered up all their belongings, they looked around for their driver. But this is where our story takes a twist—the driver was nowhere to be seen. A little surprised but definitely not alarmed, they assumed he was taking a nap. Anyhow, the enterprising Kaptaan Sahib, along with another gentleman, Mr S.K. Sharma, went off to search for him. It wasn't too difficult. The two of them did find him, resting against a pine tree and smiling benignly at the world.

Now here you must understand the psychology of our wonderful paharhiyas. They are generally happy, contented people. All they need is abundant sunshine, along with tea and the occasional beedi. Of course, a soft drink, appropriately fermented, is always welcome as a bonus. That's all they need. And since they are happy, friendly people, at peace with themselves and their lot in life, they tend to smile benignly at the world around them. Which explains why Hukam Singh was smiling benignly at the world.

'Hukam Singh, *chalo, vaapas jaane ka* time *ho gaya hai*,' said Kaptaan Sahib. But Hukam Singh continued to smile benignly at him, without moving an inch. A little irritated,

Kaptaan Sahib repeated himself. Hukam Singh merely nodded, settled even more comfortably in the nook of the tree, and smiled benignly once again.

By now Kaptaan Sahib was getting angry. He moved closer, and was about to give Hukam Singh a good shaking, when suddenly he stopped. And sniffed. And then sniffed again. And then he stepped back as if he had been slapped. 'My God, this man is drunk. Dead drunk!'

Kaptaan Sahib and Sharmaji stared at each other, aghast. And then hurried back to the rest of the picnickers. 'Our driver is drunk. There is no way he can drive us back on hill roads. That too, with darkness setting in.'

The euphoria of the picnic evaporated, as if by magic. Irrelevant questions started coming up. 'Where had he got it from?' 'Was he carrying it in the bus?' 'Could he have bought it locally?' 'How could he possibly do such a stupid thing?' Now I'm sure you would agree that these were completely meaningless questions at this stage. The key issue was, what should the revellers do now?

'What about taking a bus back?' said one of the party. 'Virtually impossible,' said someone else gloomily. This is an unimportant road, and we won't get any bus till the next morning. And to get to the main road, we'll have to walk five kilometres.' So that was the end of that silly suggestion.

'Can any one of us drive this van?' asked one of the members tentatively. There was no response. Quite understandably. After all, how many people, other than professional drivers, are able to drive a van? Incidentally, Kaptaan Sahib was a good driver, but unfortunately he had injured himself and was in no condition to drive for a few days.

By now, the fun and frolic of the picnic was completely gone, with gloom replacing it. Comments like, 'How will we get home?' Or 'My children will be desperately worried.' Or 'I had to go to a party tonight—how can I face my friends.' Or even 'There is no signal here. Why did we come to such a desolate place? How will I inform my family?' Yes dear reader, there was gloom all around. No, gloom is too mild a word. There was abject fear. Fear of ending up sleeping on the hillside all night. With bears and panthers on the prowl. What a chilling prospect!

But of course, the picnickers had reckoned without the leadership qualities of Kaptaan Sahib. In his most persuasive voice, he asked, 'Don't worry about the van—can anyone here drive a car? A private car?'

Once again there was pin drop silence. I know for a fact that there were a few souls present who *could* drive a car—although I would not have wanted to be in that car when any of them was at the wheel. However, no one was willing to risk driving the van. On hill roads, and in the darkness. There were simpler and far less painful ways to commit suicide.

Suddenly, one of the members turned to Kumar, the youngest and most meek member of the lot. 'Kumar, I had once seen you driving a car. Which means that you *can* drive.'

At this, Kumar looked around at the surrounding pine trees, trying desperately to find one that was thick enough to hide him. 'Well actually, I had got a learner's licence, but could not clear the final test. Now even that licence has expired. And I definitely cannot drive a van.' By the way, if you've never seen desperation in a human being's eyes, you should have seen Kumar at that moment. Terror is probably too mild a word for it. He was a poor driver, and he knew it. He had begun learning on a tiny Maruti car, but this one was a van. A monster of a van. There was no way he could drive it. And in a rare moment, his wife agreed with him vehemently. There was no way Kumar could be trusted with the van.

Now at this stage you might be thinking that these picnickers would have resigned themselves to their fate and that of the panthers in the forest. But then you did not know Kaptaan Sahib. Our very own Kaptaan Sahib was a true leader in the same mould as lesser luminaries such as Barack Obama, Bill Gates, and Ratan Tata. It was simply a cruel twist of fate that these other gentlemen had got the recognition that was due to them, whereas Kaptaan Sahib had not.

So Kaptaan Sahib got into the act. He coaxed and cajoled Kumar. He used all his motivational skills. He played on Kumar's pride. He even told him (Kumar) that he (Kumar) would become a hero, and that he (Kaptaan Sahib) would propose his (Kumar's) name for president of the Aaraampur club, which he (Kaptaan Sahib) had never done for anyone else, and that he (Kumar) would be able to set the vision for the club, along with him (Kaptaan Sahib) of course.

Under the onslaught of this truly motivational speech, Kumar began to relent. More so, because he could see no way out, and he did not want to end up on the dining table of the panther's family that night. One final push by Kaptaan Sahib, and the deal was sealed. Kumar—the heroic Kumar—would drive them all home in the van.

Quickly, everyone got into the van—praying all the while. Hukam Singh was dragged in as well. Without offering any resistance, and smiling benignly as always. Kumar got into the driver's seat and looked around nervously, gingerly feeling all the knobs and switches as if they were part of the crown jewels and were likely to fall apart at any moment. Fortunately however, they did not fall apart. Carefully, ever so carefully, he pushed the starter knob as though he were touching a porcupine in full bloom. With a roar, the diesel engine started, and the van was all set to move.

As you can imagine, making this journey was perhaps the most difficult thing Kumar had ever done in his life. He hung on to the steering wheel for dear life, hoping that it would save him. The winding roads were no help, and several times the van lurched to within a few inches of the valley below, leading the passengers to gasp in horror. Of course, that did nothing for Kumar's confidence, which was already at rock bottom, and plummeting further all the time. But somehow, he managed to hang on without losing any passenger (remember, this is a funny book, not a tragedy). And the nightmare continued . . .

And what about Hukam Singh? No change. He sat in the last seat of the van, smiling benignly as before. Even the glares that he got from the others from time to time made no difference. No sir, Hukam Singh was as happy as any man with a bottle of alcohol inside him can be.

All of a sudden, however, God decided to test Kumar's skills even more. The heavens opened up and it started drizzling. Darkness had set in by now, and with the added effect of the rains, visibility was at an all-time low. But our brave Kumar hung on desperately. After all, his instinct for survival was as strong as that of any one of us. With the help of the torch in Kaptaan Sahib's phone, he was able to see the road ahead for all of twenty feet. But he was grateful even for this. Slowly, ever so slowly, the van lurched along, with the passengers holding their collective breaths and praying to whichever God they believed in.

Till at last they reached the Aaraampur club. And then Kumar switched off the engine and breathed a HUGE sigh of relief—a sigh that could be heard on the other side of the mountain. His job was done.

You can imagine what happened next. Everyone crowded around Kumar. They shook hands with him and slapped him on the back. In one voice, they all said that Kumar was a hero—of the kind that Aaraampur had never seen before. I am told by a friend that had Kumar been slightly better looking, they might even have kissed him. They all invited Kumar home for dinner—invitations that he accepted gratefully. You see, his wife was one of the worst cooks in town.

So that was the end of the most eventful picnic in the history of Aaraampur. Of course, it went down into the folklore of the town, and will be passed on in hushed whispers from generation to generation.

But before I end this story, there are three things I need to tell you.

First of all, Kaptaan Sahib believed he was the real hero—the one who had saved the day. After all, that idiot Kumar would never have driven the van without his leadership. Sadly however, no one else agreed with him, and the halo that he so richly deserved, eluded him.

Secondly, I have heard from reliable sources that Kumar had to take tranquilizers every night for the next month. And when he did fall into a troubled sleep, he dreamt that he was in the driver's seat of the van with a panther sitting next to him, sizing him up for his next meal. And then of course, he woke up in a cold sweat. Yes, dear reader, poor Kumar went through the same nightmare every night for a full month.

And finally, what of Hukam Singh? Well, the picnickers had abandoned him in the van. Fortunately, his home was close by, and when he did not appear for dinner, his wife strode up to the club to reclaim her husband. She saw his face, immediately realized what had happened (it was not a new occurrence, you see), and gave him two resounding slaps on his face. Startled, Hukam Singh meekly followed her home. And finally—yes finally—the benign look on his face gave way to something closer to worry.

And that, my friend, is the story of the most famous picnic the town of Aaraampur had ever seen.

7

Jalebirams and the Mahaaa Bhatura

Before I forget, I must tell you the story of Jalebirams, the most famous *halwai* in Aaraampur. Founded several years ago by the venerable Jalebi Ram. Alas, this gentleman had passed away, and the business was handed down to his son, Barfi Das, as all family heirlooms are. And finally, passed on to *his* son, Gulab J. Chand, popularly known as Gulab ji. I'm not too sure what the letter 'J' in his name stood for, but given the family business, I can hazard a guess. Anyhow, Jalebirams was well known across the length and breadth of the district. Far, far more than the lesser-known Taj Palace hotel in Delhi, the Oberois in Mumbai, or even the Windsor Manor in Bangalore (most of the gentry in Aaraampur had not heard of these mini-hotels in any case). Whenever the wonderful folk of Aaraampur wanted to experience fine dining at its culinary best, well, they would look no further than Jalebirams. And no visitor from outside the town could leave without the mandatory visit to Jalebirams. Rather like the Taj Mahal in Agra, in case you've heard of it!

Now as you are aware, the best culinary brands always pride themselves on that one dish. That one special dish, which sets them truly apart from the riff-raff. And in the case of Jalebirams, it was their *bhatura*. I'm sure you know what a bhatura is. I'm not going to explain silly things like this. Anyhow, the bhaturas at Jalebirams were something else. Crisp on the outside and ultra-soft on the inside. Dripping with that ingredient that is mandatory in any halwai preparation—desi ghee. I've been to Jalebirams several times, and boy, I can't even begin to describe how yummy these bhaturas are.

Anyhow, before I get carried away eulogizing these bhaturas, let's get back to life in Aaraampur, which was carrying on as usual. One fine day, however, the winds of change began to blow. When our very own Kaptaan Sahib came over to Jalebirams. You see, Gulab ji was doing well. No doubt about it. But he wanted to do even better. He had been hearing young men and women talk about influencer marketing, social media marketing, and loyalty programmes. Some people also spoke about the four Ps of marketing, while devouring his bhaturas. And Gulab ji was beginning to think that he was getting left out. You see, he ran his business the way his father and grandfather had before him.

But somewhere, at the back of his head, he felt that he needed to understand these new techniques and use them. Often, he would sit back in his halwai shop, and think about what he could do. And that is how Kaptaan Sahib found him, absentmindedly chewing the leathery part of a bhatura.

'*Aao,* Kaptaan Sahib,' said Gulab ji, effusively. '*Chhole bhature?*'

Kaptaan Sahib shook his head. He had had a heavy breakfast and could not possibly eat more. But tea was welcome, and he said so.

With a delighted nod, Gulab ji told his staff to make special tea, with extra sugar. '*Ispecial insaan ke liye,*' he said, with a beaming smile.

And then the story came out, as Gulab ji shared his innermost thoughts, and asked Kaptaan Sahib if he could help. Now you are aware of how helpful Kaptaan Sahib was—you've already seen him at his helpful best when advising Pahalwaan ji. Plus, in his earlier avatar (the one he had donned before he came to Aaraampur), he had spent a fair amount of time in marketing. As expected therefore, he promptly sat down with his cup of tea, and the two of them got into a major strategy session.

Cup after cup of tea went down the two throats, as the respective minds worked feverishly. Accompanied by the occasional *barfi*—after all, Kaptaan Sahib could not keep saying no, could he? Gradually, the contours of a wonderful marketing campaign began to emerge. Kaptaan Sahib advised Gulab ji to create excitement around his brand. And after the fifth glass of highly sweetened tea, the '*Mahaaa Bhatura*' was launched.

Ah, the Mahaaa Bhatura. A bhatura that was larger than anything that had ever adorned a dining table. Massive was not the word for it. It was as large as the huge *kadhai* in which it was made. Even looking at it made you a bit scared—just in case you were called upon to eat it. However, the Mahaaa Bhatura was only a part of the story. Along with it was a challenge thrown to the good townsfolk of Aaraampur, 'Eat a full Mahaaa Bhatura in one sitting, and for one month you can eat anything at Jalebirams. Absolutely free.'

Now when this challenge was thrown, you can imagine the earthquake that shook our sleepy little town. People stopped going wherever it was they were going to, and landed up at Jalebirams. Young courting couples stopped courting in the local parks and shifted their venue to Jalebirams. Retired men stopped gossiping on the road and started gossiping at Jalebirams instead. And I'm sure you can guess the natural corollary. These people would not just sit at Jalebirams. They would eat. They would eat *rasgullas,* or *gulab jamuns*, or *samosas,* or even *bhaturas.* Not Mahaaa Bhaturas—don't be silly— just the ordinary ones.

Yes, business was great. And was Gulab ji beaming? You bet. Standing behind the counter where all the *mithai* was displayed, with his proud paunch bobbing up and down, he kept gazing fondly at the poster that his daughter had put up in the shop:

Ours Specalty

MAHAAA BHATURA
Biggestest bhatura in whole Himachal

Eat it together, and enjay all Jalebirams free for 1
month

You see, Gulab ji had a daughter called Imarti Kumari,
who had studied all the way up to class 8. English
medium, of course. Quite naturally, when promotional
material had to be designed for any campaign, she was
the chief designer-cum-copywriter. It is quite another
issue that Kaptaan Sahib, who spoke impeccable English,
blanched when he saw this poster, but that's a subject for
another book.

Now there were enough young men who would rise
to the bait and take up the challenge. Yes, there were lots
who tried, but none who succeeded. Many of them were
able to reach the halfway mark, but had to give up after
that—usually after offloading the half that they had eaten,
just outside the shop.

So no one had succeeded in this unique venture so
far. Despite this however, there was always a nagging
doubt in Gulab ji's mind. What if someone *did* manage
to eat the Mahaaa Bhatura? He would then become a free
customer for the entire month. And Gulab ji shuddered at
the impact such an event would have on his profitability.

Of course, his mentor Kaptaan Sahib had assured him that there was no such possibility, and that no human being alive could eat that massive bhatura in one sitting. And as the days went by and more and more young men fell by the wayside, Gulab ji's confidence grew.

However, like all other tales, this one has a twist as well. One day, Kaptaan Sahib spoke to his family about the wonderful campaign he had designed. And that's when Panju suddenly perked up. Kaptaan Sahib's younger son, as I've mentioned earlier, who was a student at the famous Popular Public School. Now, I must tell you that Panju was a sportsman. Revered by all the girls both in and out of school. And envied by all the boys. For his academics, did you say? Come on, don't be silly. Panju didn't care two hoots about academics. Football was his passion. And cricket. And billiards. And acting in plays. And riding his smart racing bicycle. And . . .

But most of all, Panju's passion was food. My God, you should have seen him devouring rotis when he got down to lunch. Or dinner. Anyhow, on that fateful night when Kaptaan Sahib described his campaign at Jalebirams, Panju suddenly stopped chewing his nth roti, 'What did you say, Papa?'

Kaptaan Sahib was a bit surprised. Panju had never shown any interest in his father's extensive consulting practice. However, he repeated what he had said. That is when he saw a gleam in Panju's eyes. And realized that his son had taken up the challenge.

The next day was Sunday, so there was no school. In any case, Panju was preoccupied and had no time to bother about stupid things like education. He called up three of his friends and asked them to meet him at Jalebirams at 1 p.m. sharp. Yes sir, the challenge was well and truly on.

Taking a deep breath, Panju entered the shop, and spoke to Gulab ji, '*Namaste* Gulab ji.' And then he turned to a waiter, '*Bhai*, Mahaaa Bhature *ki ek* photo *toh dikha do*.' No, don't get me wrong. Panju was supremely confident. But it never hurt to know the size and strengths of the adversary. To date he had never lost, but you never knew. . .

However, the waiter smiled politely, 'Sorry sir, *hum dikha nahin sakte hain. Aapko* order *karna hoga*.'

The tiniest of doubts now began to enter Panju's mind. Not major doubts mind you—just teeny-weeny ones. What if it turned out to be beyond his capacity? After all, he had a reputation to protect. And what would the girls in Aaraampur say, if he couldn't meet the challenge?

But by now a few other friends had joined in and were egging him on. 'Come on Panju', 'We know you can do it, Panju', '*Dikha de inko*,' and other allied motivational speeches filled the air. Perhaps even Mahatma Gandhi would never have demonstrated the kind of convincing skills that his friends displayed. With the waiters watching with bated breath, along with the venerable owner, Gulab ji. *What would the young man decide? Would he chicken out? Or would he step into the ring?* The suspense was becoming unbearable. Till finally, Panju took one final deep breath, '*Izzat ka sawaal hai, doston*.' And with that he turned to the waiter, '*Le aao*.'

There were claps all around, as the waiter turned to get the order. Even the other customers turned their

heads at the commotion. And within ten minutes, the
Mahaaa Bhatura arrived at the table.

My God, the Mahaaa Bhatura was truly something
else. It came in a huge *thali*—no plate was large enough
to hold it. But that's not all. It extended way beyond
the thali. No one had ever seen anything like it before.
Panju's eyes bulged as he looked down, and once again
doubts began to surface in his otherwise supremely
confident mind. His friends frankly stared. '*Nahin kha
sakega*', '*Rehne de*, Panju', '*Mat* try *kar yaar, mar jayega*',
were some of the motivational remarks that came his
way. But after a brief battle with his self-doubts, Panju
decided to go ahead. '*Izzat ka sawaal hai, bhai,*' saying
which he proceeded to take an experimental bite. And
with the gauntlet having been thrown down, the battle
between Panju and the Mahaaa Bhatura had well and
truly begun.

Panju was not a particularly fast eater, but he was
steady. 'Chomp, chomp' went his jaws, rarely speeding up
or slowing down, as he repeatedly bit into his adversary.
But of course, the adversary refused to relent, mocking
him all the time.

Slowly, ever so slowly, the adversary began to show
signs of wear and tear. The first milestone was reached
without too much fuss. In other words, a quarter of the
Mahaaa Bhatura had gone went down Panju's alimentary
canal. Now you should have noticed the other customers
in the restaurant. This was something new, and they were
intrigued. Some of the more adventurous ones actually
started cheering every bite that our friend Panju took.

That was just the encouragement Panju needed to move on. The chomping continued, although at a more measured pace. After all, there was a limit to human capacity—even Panju's capacity for gluttony. Slowly and steadily however, Panju managed to finish half the bhatura. Yes sir, half that mammoth bhatura had actually gone down into his digestive tract. And Panju showed no signs of stopping.

By now the excitement in the entire *halwai's* shop was at a fever pitch. Everyone there realized that something significant was about to happen. Someone even considered contacting the *Guinness Book of Records*. On second thoughts, perhaps *Ripley's Believe It or Not* might be a better place. Anyhow, prudence dictated that they wait for the last bite. After all, neither the Guinness Book nor Ripley's was likely to publish a story titled, 'Young Indian student eats half a Mahaaa Bhatura'. They would need the full thing. And so, everyone waited with bated breath . . .

It is also interesting to note the reaction of the waiters at this stage. All of them realized that they might be witness to history in the making. Quite naturally, they stopped taking orders, and simply surrounded the table where Panju and his friends were sitting. And did the other customers mind? Of course not! They were equally excited and stopped their chewing to focus on Panju and his legendary jaws. Which went on and on . . .

Now at this stage, if you were to take a look at Gulab ji, you would have noticed a frown on his face. Not outright worry, you see, but just a nagging doubt. No one had ever gone beyond this stage. Could this young man possibly eat the whole thing? Logically of course, that was impossible. No human being in his right mind—or stomach—could. But still, there was a nagging doubt that refused to go away, because this particular human being showed no sign of slowing down or giving up.

Till only one quarter of the bhatura was left. Believe it or not, Panju—our very own Panju—had managed to devour three-quarters of the humongous Mahaaa Bhatura. And then pandemonium broke out amongst the spectators. Their own miserable little samosas and gulab jamuns forgotten, all of them thronged to Panju's table. Cries of 'Come on Panju', 'You can do it Panju,' 'Yay, yay Panju,' filled the air. Phones were brought out and videos were taken. And you should have seen Panju. His breathing was just a little bit laboured, his eyes were slightly—only slightly—glassy, but he was in no mood to give up. Not now, after having reached so close to the finish line.

By now word had spread through Aaraampur at lightning speed. Social media, you know. Not since Neeraj Chopra won his historic Olympic gold medal, had WhatsApp groups in Aaraampur been this busy. I'm told that in the USA, a young man named Zuckerberg was worried about his server crashing. Anyway, as the word spread, the good townsfolk of Aaraampur made a beeline for Jalebirams. Those who couldn't get space, simply stood outside, sipping their tea and biting into their samosas. And everyone was on their feet, cheering every morsel that went down. Waiters, customers, everyone.

Except for Gulab ji, who was, frankly, panicking by now. Quietly, without anyone noticing, he called out to one of the waiters and whispered something to him. The waiter scurried away but returned in five minutes with a plate of crisp samosas in his hand. He brought it to Panju's table, and asked him with a beaming smile, 'Would you like some samosas, sir? On the house—you won't have to pay for them.' By the way, in case you had noticed, you would have seen Gulab ji hovering around in the background, almost praying . . .

Panju looked up from his steady chomping. The samosas were golden brown in colour and looked terribly inviting. But obviously he wasn't fooled by the trick. 'Yes but let me finish the bhatura first.'

And what do you think finally happened? You're right, my friend—Panju actually managed to put the last bite of the Mahaaa Bhatura into his mouth, chewed it, looked around and swallowed it. And that was the signal for the entire shop to erupt; 'Panju, Panju,' shouted everyone, clapping, cheering and slapping him on his back. All except Gulab ji, who was desperately trying to hide in a dark corner of the shop.

But Panju wasn't finished yet. '*Now* get me the samosas,' he said to the waiter, in his most magnanimous tone. And proceeded to demolish them before the horrified onlookers. While Gulab ji groaned and cursed his luck. Never again would he listen to Kaptaan Sahib's advice.

And with that, our episode of Panju and the Mahaaa Bhatura came to an end. But there is more, so please read on . . .

A couple of days later, two of Panju's friends landed up at Jalebirams. They walked in, looked around, and stared. Yes, they simply stared. The earlier poster was nowhere to be seen. But in its place, there was a brand new one. Which looked like this:

New Chalenj

MAHAAA BHATURA
Biggestest bhatura in whole Himachal

Break Panju's record of 48 minutes

And enjay all Jalebirams free for 1 month

You see, Kaptaan Sahib was a marketing whiz. At least *he* thought so, and his wife did not disagree with him. The new challenge was his idea. Panju had taken 48 minutes to eat the Mahaaa Bhatura, so why not ask everyone else to try and break his record? Incidentally, I'm told that he now has an offer from the Marriott hotel group, as their marketing consultant.

And what about the girls in Aaraampur? Well, some of them were truly impressed. Every time they passed Panju, they looked at him with something close to devotion in their eyes. But then there were others who simply said, 'Ugh, how disgusting. What an animal!' But of course, Panju didn't mind—after all it took all sorts to make this world.

Finally, let's also look at what happened to Panju himself. It is a documented fact that after this particular episode, he didn't have his dinner, or even breakfast the next day. But by lunchtime you could have seen him as usual, putting away the same massive helpings of roti and dal.

Yes ladies and gentlemen, our friend Panju had returned to normal.

And so had life at Aaraampur . . .

8

Smoking Is Injurious to Your Health

I've already told you that our friend Kaptaan Sahib had migrated to the sleepy little town of Aaraampur, to pursue a career in farming. Now, it's time to introduce you to his partner in this noble venture—a younger person named Anand. Between them, Kaptaan Sahib and Anand took up a piece of land on lease beyond Kalaghat, around 14 kilometres from Aaraampur, where there they tried out scientific methods of farming. After all, they were both well-educated. They grew mushrooms and off-season vegetables. They even experimented with organic farming. And . . .

But hang on. What they grew is not really of interest to us here. What *is* of interest is their habits. You see, both Kaptaan Sahib and Anand were dedicated smokers. I would go as far as to say that the tobacco industry in India was booming because of people like them. Their wives hated it. Their children hated it. But they themselves loved it, and therefore they wouldn't stop.

As you might imagine, from time to time, Kaptaan Sahib and Anand would need to stay on the farm for a few days at a stretch. And in the evening, after a hard day's work, the two partners would switch on their TV, light one cigarette after another, sit back, and watch the latest T20 cricket match. Pure relaxation, if you know what I mean.

One day however, they happened to switch to a channel where a doctor was speaking. This doctor was talking about the harmful effects of smoking. Idly, the two listened to this doctor. And then something quite fascinating happened. You see, this doctor was a terrific speaker. And—very, very convincing. Perhaps even very, very, VERY convincing. And our two partners were very, very, VERY convinced. Yes, dear reader, after years and years of lectures on the subject by their families, their doctors, and even the neighbourhood *kirana* shop owner (who did not sell cigarettes, so there was no conflict of interest), it finally took a TV programme to do the job. They looked at each other, nodded briefly, and that was it. Both of them decided to give up smoking. Not tomorrow, not the next week, but THEN AND THERE. Of course, before implementing this glorious plan, they finished the cigarettes they were currently smoking. After all, they couldn't waste money, could they?

Now if you think that was it, you did not know these two gentlemen. They were clear that God had sent them down to earth with a mission. And just giving up smoking themselves was too trivial to be their mission. Having taken this decision, they had to spread their message worldwide. However, a few cigarettes later, they realized that this was perhaps a wee bit ambitious. For instance, how could they possibly convince people in South America to quit smoking? They didn't even know the language. And so, in a series of steps they brought down their canvas to India, the state of Himachal, the town of Aaraampur, and finally to the village of Kalaghat, where their farm was located. Yes, that was just perfect. They would ensure that all the menfolk in the village gave up smoking. And that would be a major, major step towards the mission that God had entrusted them with.

Having taken this earth-shattering decision, they lit one last cigarette (just to seal the deal, you see) and got into action. All the men of the village were promptly called over, and they faithfully came. Kaptaan Sahib and Anand then expounded on their newest favourite subject (there had been others, typically changing on a weekly basis, but this was the real thing, you see). Our two partners were almost as convincing as the doctor on TV, and the villagers were well and truly convinced. In any case, these two men had completed their school education, and for our villagers that was the clincher. They looked upon the two 'baujis' as the fountainhead of knowledge and were willing to follow them blindly.

Now the iron was hot. Red hot. And our two partners decided that this was the right time to strike. '*Apne ghar mein jitni beedi-*cigarette *hain, sab le aao,*' they said in a commanding voice. At which, the villagers scurried away. After all, Bauji had spoken. And promptly returned with bundles of beedis. After which Kaptaan Sahib lit a bonfire and proceeded to throw two packets of cigarettes into it, saying, '*Yeh hamari* cigarette *hain. Dekho, hamne chhodh di. Ab aap log bhi aag mein daalo.*'

The villagers were shocked. Their beloved, hard-earned beedis! How could they possibly throw them into the bonfire? But then again, Bauji had spoken and that too, the senior Bauji, who was all-knowing. Suddenly the most daring of the villagers threw his precious bundle of beedis into the bonfire. Another followed, and then another. And then all hell broke loose. Bundles of beedis were flung into the bonfire as a kind of catharsis, as the villagers sat around the bonfire and watched them go up in smoke. At the end, everyone took a vow never to smoke again, and went back home to break the good news to their respective wives. As you can imagine, the wives were delighted, and soon after, a delegation of women came over to meet Kaptaan Sahib and Anand. Just to thank them for the miraculous change that had come over their respective husbands.

That night passed peacefully, and then it was morning. Kaptaan Sahib woke up and reached out for his usual packet. But of course, it had been consumed by the bonfire yesterday. Groggily he remembered yesterday's steely resolve and pulled his hand away. That day passed off with a lot of longing and some regret. 'Just one cigarette' was all he wanted. By the way, Anand was in exactly the same position. Now, don't get me wrong. Neither of them wanted to start smoking again—they were convinced about the dangers of the habit. But what was the harm in just one . . .?

That evening Kaptaan Sahib and Anand were not their usual cheerful self. In fact, they were extremely irritable. And the night was even worse. They probably didn't sleep all night. And in the morning, when Kaptaan Sahib woke up, he was thinking. And then thinking some more. And finally, he reached his decision. Quietly, ever so quietly, he asked Anand, '*Yaar, koi* cigarette *bachi hai?*'

Anand was relieved. He had had exactly the same withdrawal pangs as Kaptaan Sahib, but he wouldn't make the first move. He reached under his bed with a knowing smile and brought out two, half-broken cigarettes. '*Bacha key rakkhi theen.*'

Kaptaan Sahib's eyes lit up, and his whole body started quivering. Half-broken they might be, but they were wonderful, wonderful cigarettes. The two colleagues lit their cigarettes and inhaled deeply. What bliss! How could they ever have made such a stupid decision? No way. They COULD NOT and WOULD NOT give up smoking. And to hell with what the doctor said. He was probably a chain-smoker himself. With that, the transformation in reverse was complete, and our partners returned to their earlier happy state.

But our story does not end there. What about the poor villagers—those who had thrown their beedis into the bonfire? How could Kaptaan Sahib and Anand possibly face these villagers? So the two made a pact. They would never smoke in the open—only in secret, within the confines of the little farmhouse that they stayed in.

Alas, secrets rarely remain secrets for long. Two days later, one of the villagers was walking past the open window of their farmhouse, when he smelt smoke. 'Cigarette? *Bauji aur* cigarette?' Not wanting to believe what he had smelt, he knocked timidly on the door of the farmhouse. Bauji opened the door and was seen frantically waving his hands around, trying to get the smoke to disappear. However, the villager was smart. *'Bauji, aap phir se . . .?'*

Bauji looked quite embarrassed, but then the villager quickly responded, *'Bauji, ham bhi nahin chhodh sake. Hamne bhi dobaara shuru kar li.'*

Greatly relieved, Kaptaan Sahib offered him a puff, which he accepted gratefully. And then the whole story came out. Apparently, after that momentous decision around the bonfire, every smoker in the village had had severe second thoughts. And had gone back to smoking in the privacy of their homes so as not to offend the two Baujis.

That evening, all the men of the village gathered outside Bauji's farmhouse. Around a bonfire. With lit beedis once again. But this time the beedis were in their mouths, and not in the bonfire. Yes sir, these men had taken a solemn pledge. Never again would they take such an idiotic, meaningless pledge. Inhaling deeply, the group was as close to nirvana as humanly possible. And with that, the village of Kalaghat had returned to normal.

But before I end, there is a bit more to tell you. I have a friend who works with ITC, the giant cigarette manufacturer. A few months after this episode, I happened to meet this friend. And he recounted an interesting experience, 'You know, we barely managed to avert a strong anti-smoking movement, which had started off in a little village of Himachal, but which threatened to affect the entire country. Thank God—that would have been the end of the tobacco industry,' he finished and looked relieved.

'Do you remember the name of the village?' I asked.

'I think it was something like Kalagaon. Or maybe Kalaghora. No, I think it was Kalaghat. Yes, definitely Kalaghat. Why? Are you aware of what happened?'

Of course, I merely looked at him and smiled. But till this day, I haven't told him why.

9

Doctor Sahib

And now I must tell you about the time Doctor Sahib came to Aaraampur. Yes my friend, that was a truly historic day for our sleepy little hill town. There were already some doctors in town (I believe you've met Dr Sood, the psychiatrist), but this gentleman was the real thing. Extremely impressive in his white coat, with a stethoscope sitting proudly across his neck, one look at Doctor Harish Lamba (for that was his name) was enough to set the patient's confidence soaring. I would go so far as to say that this was half the treatment for whichever malady the patient was suffering from.

But that's enough meandering. Let's get down to the story. As I have said, one fine summer's day the good residents of Aaraampur woke up to see a bright yellow board on top of what had earlier been a kirana shop.

Proudly proclaiming, 'Dr Harish Lamba, MBBS'. With a huge '+' on either side of the name. My God, how impressive it looked. Yes, the erstwhile kirana shop was gone (obvious, isn't it), to be replaced by a spanking new clinic that even the residents of Delhi would have been proud of. Behind the cabin door sat Dr Lamba, absolutely reeking of medical knowledge, if that were possible. Outside the cabin sat his compounder, whose job it was to create the concoctions that Dr Sahib prescribed in his occasionally decipherable handwriting.

And did the public come? You bet they did. They came in droves. From the town of Aaraampur, from nearby villages, even from far-flung locales such as Theog and Jutogh. Such was the deluge of patients at Dr Sahib's clinic, that you might have wondered if all the ailments of the world were concentrated in the town of Aaraampur and its environs. Yes, Dr Lamba was kept totally busy from early morning (11 a.m.) to a hurried lunch (12.30 p.m.), and once again in the evening (6.30 p.m.) till he retired for the day, utterly exhausted (7.30 p.m.). Aaraampur had rarely seen the likes of such a hardworking gentleman. Of course, the fact that paharhi genes come with an antidote to hard work had nothing to do with it.

Anyhow, to continue with our story, one day our good old Kaptaan Sahib came to the clinic, accompanied by Ram Lal, one of his farm hands, and his young son. Now here's the twist—Kaptaan Sahib's fourth cousin was a doctor. Yes, you heard that right. He was a doctor, and Kaptaan Sahib had picked up some medical tips from him. Obviously, this scattered knowledge was nothing compared to that of the real practitioner sitting on the other side of the table. Anyhow, the boy's eyeballs had turned slightly yellowish, and unfortunately he had been throwing up. Based on his phenomenal medical knowledge, Kaptaan Sahib thought it was jaundice, and so would any of us with even the remotest idea about medical science. However, it was the doctor's decision. Quick as a wink, he examined the boy using his stethoscope almost like a scimitar. Then he checked his pulse, his tongue, and all other parts of the body that were available to be checked. Then, in a tone that might have reminded you of King Solomon several centuries ago, he pronounced his judgement, '*Gala kharaab hai.*'

Kaptaan Sahib was surprised. The boy had not complained of any pain in the throat. Not wanting to offend the doctor, he offered, 'Doctor Sahib, *kahin* jaundice *toh nahin hai?*'

You can imagine the reaction of our good doctor to this affront to his medical knowledge. Bristling with indignation, he said in a loud and clear voice, '*Daktar kaun hai, aap ya hum? Aur kuchh bhi ho*, jaundice *toh hai hi nahin.*' And with this contemptuous dismissal of our Kaptaan's opinion, he turned to write out the prescription. Utterly confused by now, Kaptaan Sahib kept his silence. After all, you couldn't argue with a famous medical practitioner, could you? And so, an appropriate antibiotic was prescribed for the throat.

A week later, the symptoms were no better. If anything, they were worse. And quite naturally, Kaptaan Sahib, along with the father-son duo, landed up at the doctor's clinic once again. By now, it was a frank case of jaundice. And what do you think the doctor said? '*Yeh, ek* rare type *ka* jaundice *hai, jo shuru mein dikhta nahin hai. Par fikar mat karo, maine aise bahuton ka ilaaj kiya hai.*' Saying which, he promptly knocked out the antibiotic and prescribed the appropriate medicine for jaundice.

Now at this moment, you should have seen Ram Lal's face. Devotion was perhaps too mild a term for what he felt right now. '*Hum kitne khush kismat hain. Daktar Sahib ne aisi mushkil bimari ko bhi pakad liya.*' Touching the doctor's feet reverentially, he went out with his son.

However, if you had noticed Kaptaan Sahib's face as he went out, you would say that he was thinking. . .

Fortunately, the boy recovered, and the doctor's reputation spread even further if that was possible. Here was a doctor who was able to diagnose and treat rare diseases. Now the reader might be aware that there is no real cure for jaundice—all that is required is rest and an appropriate diet. No *chhola* bhaturas, no *pooris*, and definitely no *paranthas*. But that, of course, is irrelevant to our story. The key thing is that Dr Lamba had successfully diagnosed and treated a rare form of jaundice. And for that, the citizens of Aaraampur were deeply indebted to him.

A few days later, Kaptaan Sahib visited him again— this time with his gardener who had loose motions. The doctor promptly prescribed some tablets and the two went away. However, just three days later, they came back, with Kaptaan Sahib looking angry, and the gardener desperately clutching his stomach. 'Doctor Sahib, loose motion *bahut zyaada ho gayi hai.*' The doctor looked at the tablet, and roared, '*Yeh toh galat dawai hai.*'

Utterly cowed, the poor patient whispered, because that was all he could do in his current state, '*Par Daktar Sahib, aapne yehi dawai likhi thi.*' The doctor checked the prescription. It was true. This was the medicine he had prescribed. But obviously, he couldn't admit it, 'Chemist *ne galat dawai de di,*' was all he said accusingly, and promptly changed the prescription.

Over the next few weeks, incidents such as the ones I have just described kept taking place with monotonous regularity. And over time, they began to take a bit of a toll on the doctor's reputation. Nothing significant, mind you—most of the residents of Aaraampur still had immense faith in the doctor. The fault lay with the patient for not taking the right dose, or the chemist for giving out the wrong medicine, or even the disease— which was probably rare and therefore no medical practitioner could be expected to diagnose it and treat it at first go. Yes sir, these people had phenomenal faith in our good doctor.

But there were a few idiots who were beginning to have doubts. 'Why was his diagnosis wrong so often?' 'Why did he prescribe the wrong medicine, and then blame the chemist?' 'Why did so many patients get worse after meeting him?' Of course, these people were in a minority. However, what is more interesting is the behaviour of these people. Believe it or not, these few non-believers started visiting the compounder for their ailments, and over time this gentleman build up a thriving side business. After the doctor had left for the day, naturally.

One fine day, the bubble burst. It had to! You see, the Kaptaans' maid's son had fallen down and injured his foot. Bleeding profusely, he was taken to Dr Lamba, who promptly applied a bit of mild antiseptic and sent the boy home, with strict instructions to come back every day to get the dressing changed. The boy came back religiously every day, and the antiseptic was applied equally religiously. But for some strange reason, the wound only got worse and kept getting worse. As always, the doctor was supremely confident, '*Koi aisi beemari nahin hai jisko maine thheek na kiya ho. Yeh chhoti si chot kya cheez hai?*'

Now by sheer coincidence, during this period Kaptaan Sahib had a guest from the faraway city of Chennai—a well-known doctor named Dr C.K.R. Swamy. He took one look at the boy's wound and immediately said, 'This is bad. If we don't arrest the infection right away, the poor boy's foot will need to be amputated!' Having said this, Dr Swamy prescribed a strong dose of antibiotics, and I'm happy to inform you that within a few days, the boy recovered.

But now that Dr Swamy was around, Kaptaan Sahib was thinking. Over a drink in the evening, he happened to show him a prescription from Dr Lamba. And you should have seen Dr Swamy's reaction. He simply exploded, 'You call this a prescription? This is insane.' He then asked for a few more prescriptions made out by our friendly Aaraampur doctor. Looking at them, his face became more and more grim. Till finally he growled, 'This man is a quack. He has no business to be practising. Has anyone seen his MBBS degree?'

And that was that. The grapevine in Aaraampur, always supremely active, went into overdrive. 'Dr Lamba has a fake degree.' 'He is not a doctor. Never go to him.' Now as you are aware, rumours have a habit of self-modification as they travel. So the message changed to, 'Dr Lamba is an escaped convict. He was responsible for several murders. We are indeed fortunate that we found this out in time.' And the residents thanked the local deity for saving their lives from this murderous assassin.

And what of Dr Lamba? No one really knew what happened to him. But one bright summer's day, his clinic was back to what it earlier was—a kirana shop. And the town of Aaraampur returned to its old ways.

However, that is not the end of the story. One day, Kaptaan Sahib happened to go to Kullu—another town in Himachal—where he met an old friend. And this friend was gushing over a new doctor who had just set up his clinic in town. 'You can't imagine how good this doctor is,' he extolled.

Fearing the worst, Kaptaan Sahib asked, 'What's his name?'

'Dr Parasher,' was the immediate reply. In a truly reverent tone, as if describing an angel from heaven.

Kaptaan Sahib breathed a sigh of relief. But then his friend piped up, 'I had the honour of having a selfie taken along with this famous man. See?'

Kaptaan Sahib looked at the photograph. And yes, it was the very same Dr Lamba. The name had been changed and he had grown a beard, but the face was unmistakable.

With a sigh, Kaptaan Sahib patted his friend on the back, 'Let's go down to Ram Saran, the halwai, and pick up a cup of tea. I have something to tell you.'

10

The Unwanted Guests

One fine day the Kaptaans were enjoying a cup of tea in the little garden in front of their house. Birds were chirping nearby, and a TV could be heard in the distance. The *pakoras* in front of them were heavenly. So what if they just were a wee bit over-fried? At peace with the world and utterly relaxed, they could not possibly have asked for more.

Suddenly this peace was shattered by the arrival of Raj Kumar and his wife. Armed with two large suitcases and accompanied by their two boys, aged twelve and eight, the Kumars beamed at the Kaptaans. *'Aur yaar, kaisa hai? Bahut din se tujhe dekha nahin tha, to hamne socha aa ke mil lein.'* And with that Raj Kumar turned to Mrs Kaptaan with a bright, *'Namaste Bhabhiji.'*

Now for you to really understand this story and the ripples it caused in the Kaptaan household, I must give you the background. You see, Raj Kumar and Kaptaan Sahib were fourth cousins, which made their relationship extremely close indeed by hill standards. The Kumars lived in Theog, about a hundred kilometres from Aaraampur, and were the proud owners of a little farm. They fondly believed that they were great company, and that everyone who came in touch with them was fortunate indeed. It's another matter that everyone else thought otherwise—including the Kaptaans. They thought the Kumars were loudmouths, and spoke non-stop with just an occasional pause—after all, they had to breathe sometime. To top it all, they were extremely opinionated. Listening to Mr Kumar, one got the feeling that the country had missed something. Amongst all the prime ministers India had had, he would have been by far the best. He had a solution to every problem, all the way from population control, to the Indian economy, to Pakistan, to climate change, to . . .

And of course, his doting wife agreed with him.

Above all, they were very, very inquisitive. They would not rest till they had ferreted out all details. During their last visit, Raj Kumar had had an interrogation session with his cousin. '*Yaar, tera nat worth kya hoga* ['net worth', for the uninitiated]?' he asked. Not wanting to divulge details, Kaptaan Sahib mumbled something unintelligible and tried to change the topic. But Kumar would have none of it. '*Bataa yaar. Tu mujhe nahin batayega to kisko batayega?*' Again, Kaptaan Sahib tried to evade the issue. But his wonderful cousin was persistence personified. '*Arrey yaar, bataa de na. Achha, itna bataa de, tere paas do* crore *hain ke nahin?*' And by the way, had you been there when this interrogation was taking place, you would have noticed that the Kaptaans' maid had suddenly found something to do within earshot of this conversation, 'What juicy gossip. Wait till my friends hear this!' Even when Kaptaan Sahib asked her to go and get him a glass of water, she refused to budge. How could she possibly miss this complete disrobing of the Kaptaans' financial status?

That's right, the Kumars simply *had* to find out all details about the Kaptaan household, whether it was the Kaptaans' financial well-being, or the status of their marriage, and whether or not divorce was impending. Or even whether their cousin's niece had had a baby yet. '*Arre bhai, abhi tak nahin hua? Koi* problem *hai kya?*'

Best of all, the Kumars were always in need of money. Whether it was to buy a two-wheeler, or a brand-new LED television set, or even a microwave oven. And who else would they look to, but their friendly banker, Kaptaan Sahib. How could he possibly refuse them? And they were not asking for a dole. No way, please don't insult the Kumars. They were asking for a friendly loan. Interest-free, naturally. It is quite another matter that these loans were never returned, but believe me, the intention to return the money was always there. It was just bad luck that every time the Kumars planned to return the money, the crop at their farm failed. Or there was a theft at home. Or there was a medical emergency in the family. Of course, these unfortunate events did not stop them from taking expensive vacations, or wearing the latest branded clothes.

No sir, these were necessary expenses that were expected of a family with their kind of eminent social standing.

But wait. You haven't heard the best part yet. The crowning glory was the two young boys who accompanied them. Appropriately named Monu and Pappu, the two were ruffians of the highest order. Constantly running around, shouting and screaming, taking things apart and not being able to put them back again, and breaking roughly one item of furniture per day. And the fights! Every day brought a new round of fights between the two youngsters, with no referee. And of course, ending up in the younger boy lying on the floor, kicking, screaming and wailing in equal measure. And what did their parents say? *'Bacche hain ji. Yeh nahin karenge to aur kaun karega?'*

Having heard and assimilated these fine traits of the Kumar family, you can imagine why the Kaptaans were somewhat less than excited at prospect of spending the next few days with them. Anyhow, the Kaptaans were polite people and the Kumars were guests, so they had to be entertained. And believe me, they *did* need to be entertained. Specifically, it was their digestive systems (which proved to be extremely hardy, bottomless pits), that needed to be entertained. *'Bhabhiji, chai pila do.'* Or *'Aapke pakode yaad aa gaye.'* Or the crowning glory, *'Aapke paas wale dhabe mein* butter chicken *bahut badhiya milta hai. Chalo laate hain.'* And of course, the butter chicken and other forms of edible birds and animals had to be accompanied by liberal doses of alcohol.

You would also have realized why the nervous systems of the Kaptaans reacted most unfavourably to any visit by the Kumars. Thanks to Mr Kumar's loud and entirely unsolicited advice to the prime minister and his council of ministers, the constant loud monologues, the stream of delicacies designed to satiate the digestive juices of the Kumars, and the crash of breaking furniture, followed by the inevitable screaming and wailing of the kids. Like most paharhiyas, the Kaptaans had a robust, outstandingly calm and patient nervous system, almost to a fault (you should meet me to get a sample). But even this was beginning to fray at the edges.

Fortunately, on the eighth day of the ordeal, Mr Kumar confided to his cousin, '*Kal hamein jaana hoga.*'

Now you can well imagine Kaptaan Sahib's reaction. Every vein in his body and perhaps a few more, wanted to burst into celebration. Finally, he could see light at the end of the exasperating, frustrating, extremely noisy tunnel. But Kaptaan Sahib was a gentleman to the core, and with a major effort, he hid his delight. '*Ek do din ruk kyon nahin jaate?*'

Kumar considered this eminently reasonable request. Naturally, he had to consult his wife on this major decision with potentially international ramifications. And finally came back beaming. '*Aap kahtey ho to ruk jaate hain. Aakhir kab kab milne ka mauka milta hai?*'

And that was that. Completely aghast at what he had done, Kaptaan Sahib was reduced to venting his frustration on his favourite apricot tree. Fortunately, the apricot tree was used to these occasional outbursts, and took this tirade in its stride.

More frustration followed, till even the outstandingly patient Kaptaans could stand it no more. '*Bacchon ke* school *ki chhutti hai kya?*' This of course was said with mild sarcasm, hoping the Kumars would get the hint.

'*Nahin ji, par chhoti* class *hai na?* Miss *kar lenge. Dekho yahaan kitna 'enjay' kar rahe hain.*'

And the Kaptaans had to agree that the kids were 'enjaying' themselves very much. Too bad the Kaptaans were not. But who cared? They tried another ruse, 'Farm *pe aapki zaroorat nahin hai?*' But again, this attempt proved to be futile. '*Nahin ji.* Ram Lal (the trusted farm hand) *sambhaal lega.*' And that was that.

However, one fine, sunny day, the ordeal showed some signs of coming to an end. Two weeks after they landed up, Kumar blurted out a confession to his cousin, '*Yaar, dil to nahin karta hai, par kal jaana hi padega. Itna* school miss *nahin kara sakte hain.*'

With a tremendous effort, Kaptaan Sahib managed to suppress his upbringing and refrained from what any polite paharhiya would have said at this time. Yes sir, he did not say, '*Thoda aur ruk jao.*' Instead, he kept quiet, hoping against hope that this was the real thing. Even Kumar was quiet, expecting such an invitation. But when it did not come, he sighed, turned away, and went off muttering to himself, '*Mera bhai hai, par do din rukne ko bhi nahin bola. Kya ho gaya hai aajkal ke rishton ko?*'

The Kaptaans were on tenterhooks that night. 'Will they, won't they,' was the million-dollar question. Not wanting to build up their hopes, they spent a surprisingly quiet night. And wonder of wonders, in the morning the bags were all packed and ready. With a deep sigh of satisfaction, the Kaptaans bid the Kumars farewell. '*Phir aana, bhai sahib*,' was Mrs Kaptaan's parting shot. Fortunately, she did not see the glare she got from her husband in response.

Gradually, the Kaptaan household limped back to normal—a peaceful, quiet, blissful, Kumar-free normal. With the chirping of the birds and the distant drone of the neighbourhood television being audible once again. In the evening the Kaptaans sat in their favourite seats in their garden, putting the nightmarish past two weeks behind them. Yes, my friend, the world was at peace again.

Suddenly, they heard footsteps. And who did they see? Come on, I'm sure you've guessed by now. That's right, it was the Kumars in full glory—all four of them, plus the two suitcases. '*Hamne* Theog *phone kiya, toh pata laga ke* school *mein* headmaster *ki* death *ho gayi hai.* School *teen din tak bandh hai. To hamne socha, kyon na hum thodhe aur din ruk jayen?*'

'*Bhabhiji, pakode milenge?*'

11

Aaraampur Gets a Start-up

And now I must tell you about the time that our sleepy little town of Aaraampur was catapulted into the big league. When it was compared to Delhi, Bangalore and Chennai, in hushed whispers. Sometimes even the Silicon Valley in the USA. When discussions shifted from subjects like politics, the weather, and the latest movies, to valuations, angel investors, unicorns, and other similar exotic subjects. Yes my friend, you've guessed right. This was the time that Aaraampur got its first startup.

You see, Aaraampur boasted of several bright, young people. And one of the brightest was Nikita—or Nikki, in case you didn't want to waste time pronouncing that extra syllable. After doing her engineering from PITS, Nikki had taken up a job in the faraway city of Mumbai. The salary was good. The work was interesting. But somehow, there was something missing. She really couldn't place it, but again and again the thought came to her, 'Is this what I want to do in life?' And the thinking went on . . .

. . . when suddenly one day, while reading about how the education platform Byju's had created a mammoth from a fledgling startup, it hit her like a hammer. Then and there, her decision was made. She would create a startup. And, loyal daughter of Aaraampur that she was, the startup would be based in Aaraampur.

Nikki was so excited. She called up a couple of friends and told them the great news. Naturally, the three of them went out to celebrate over beer and other allied goodies. But that's when one of them asked her, 'Nikki, all this sounds great. But what kind of startup will you create?' And that's when the second round of thinking started. More beer, and more thinking. Still more beer, and still more thinking. When the restaurant had to shut down for the night and the manager threatened to throw the girls out, they shifted to Nikki's apartment and continued the beer and thinking over there. Many, many options were looked at and discarded. But finally, somewhere around 4 a.m. (or it may have been 4.30 a.m.—I'm not too sure), Nikki reached her second decision. You see, she had been mighty impressed with the Uber and Ola cabs in Mumbai. These companies allowed you to book a cab from an app. You could even track the cab and figure out how long it would take to reach you. And, there were no unpleasant negotiations either. Her mind went back to the times she had tried to book a taxi in Aaraampur. In some cases, the driver had been far away in a place like Dagshai or Narkanda and couldn't come. On other occasions, the phone was constantly engaged. And several times, the driver had simply refused to pick up the phone—perhaps because he was enjoying his siesta, and earning a few rupees was not on his list of priorities. Yes, booking a taxi in Aaraampur was a project in itself. You had to make multiple phone calls, and even after that there was no assurance that you would actually get one.

Nikki realized that an app-based taxi service was just what Aaraampur needed. Not just Aaraampur, but even the quaint towns and villages nearby, such as Oachghat and Subathu. And that was that. Her mind firmly made up, Nikki returned to Aaraampur to launch what she proudly called 'Aaraampur Cabs'.

Now the first thing an app-based taxi service needed was an app. Whenever a customer wanted to book a cab, the app would send out a request to all drivers in the vicinity, and one of those who responded would get the ride. To develop this app, she needed a tech co-founder. For which she caught hold of Pikki, her childhood friend, and a tech whiz. But most of all, she needed an advisor— or mentor, if you prefer the term. And who better than our very own Kaptaan Sahib?

Together, Nikki and Pikki planned out the venture. While Nikki was on the road, meeting potential customers as well as cab drivers, Pikki was at her laptop, furiously programming away. And in between, they had strategic reviews with their mentor. At Jalebirams—where else? It took a few months, but finally the great day arrived. The day when Aaraampur Cabs was launched with a lot of fanfare and the distribution of *laddoos*. Yes, ladies and gentlemen, with this service, Aaraampur had well and truly arrived on the Indian startup scene.

As you can imagine, the good citizens of Aaraampur were delighted with this new addition to their wonderful town. Suddenly, you could see Aaraampur taxis all over the place. Even if you wanted to go a couple of hundred metres away, people wouldn't walk any more. No sir, that was now considered below their dignity. They would order an Aaraampur Cab! And while getting in and getting out of the cab, they would pose for photographs with an oh-so-smug expression. Along with the smiling driver, of course. In fact, the demand for Aaraampur Cabs came in even from far-flung villages like Dharampur and Kumarhatti. Yes, my friend, Aaraampur Cabs had well and truly come to town.

However, as you are aware, in the world of business, things are never so hunky-dory. Over the next few weeks, Nikki and Pikki realized that their wonderful venture was facing problems that Uber and Ola had perhaps never heard of. For instance, when a customer tried to book a cab, the response from the drivers was often poor. In some cases, there was no response at all, and in others it came in as much as half an hour late. In addition, even after responding, some drivers would take an hour or more to reach—even though they were known to be just five minutes away. As you can imagine, this was not great for business, so they decided to seek out their mentor, Kaptaan Sahib.

The advice from Kaptaan Sahib was clear. 'Look at the data. Meet these drivers and confront them with these transactions. Figure out what's going wrong. After that we can decide what to do.'

And that's exactly what our young friends did. They took a round of Aaraampur and its adjoining areas and met these offending drivers. Starting with Soorat Ram, one of the first taxi drivers to have registered with Aaraampur Cabs.

'*Soorat Ram ji, aap ne 14 tareek ko 10 bajey* trip accept *kari thi. Par* trip *shuru hone tak* 11 *baj gaye. Kya hua?*'

Soorat Ram scratched his head, took several puffs of his beedi, and tried to remember this pre-historic fact. Suddenly his face lit up, '*Haan, maine* trip accept *kari thi. Par phir paanch mint chai peene baith gaya.*'

'*Paanch minute? Soorat Ram ji, yeh* app *ek ghanta dikha raha hai.*'

'*Haan, do char mint zyaada ho gaye honge,*' was the somewhat sheepish reply.

'*Achha, ek baat bataiye. Kisi bhi din, do se paanch baje tak aapne koi* trip accept *nahin ki. Kyon?*'

'*Woh mera soney ka time hai. Kabhi aaraam bhi karna hota hai, na?*'

Nikki and Pikki looked at each other in horror. No trips between 2 p.m. and 5 p.m.? What a disaster. Anyhow, after a few more questions, the two said namaste and moved on to the next driver.

'Madan Lal ji, *aapne teen din pehle ek* trip accept *kari thi. Par shuru karne mein dedh ghanta lag gaya. Kya baat thi?*'

Madan Lal peered at the offending data. And then suddenly his face cleared. '*Haan, mera padosi aa gaya tha. Do char mint baat karne mein lag gaye.*'

Trying to keep the frustration out of her voice, Nikki blurted out, 'Madan Lal ji, *do char* minute *nahin, dedh ghanta.*'

'*Ho sakta hai. Ek baar koi insaan aata hai, toh usko jaane mein* time *toh lagta hi hai na*?' And with that, he washed his hands of all responsibility for the crime.

'*Aur bahut saare* trips *aapne* accept *hi nahin kiye. Yeh dekhiye . . .*'

Again, Madan Lal peered at the screen of Nikki's phone, '*Kaise karta? Yeh toh sab do aur paanch baje ke beech mein* they.'

Fearing the worst, Nikki then said, '*Usse kya hota hai*?'

'*Arrey bhai, sona nahin hai maine*?'

And that was that.

Several more interviews followed, but the gist was the same. Even after a cab was booked, it could take up to an hour and a half for the trip to start. And worst of all, the time slot from 2 p.m. to 5 p.m. was sacrosanct. God had ordained that all drivers must sleep during that period, and who were these mere mortals to disobey him?

Faced with this disastrous market survey, Nikki and Pikki simply had to go back to their mentor. Almost in tears, they asked him, 'Sir, we don't know what to do. These drivers just don't take their trips seriously. They are either having endless cups of tea, or just chit chatting. In some cases, they accept the trip but turn up over an hour later. And everyone is adamant about the fact that afternoons are for naps. Sir, we can't figure out what to do.'

But of course, Kaptaan Sahib was made of sterner stuff. He had seen a lot more in life, and had battled enough adversity. And he had also seen a bit of Aaraampur since he had migrated. With a faint idea forming in his mind, he said, 'Look, so far, you've met these drivers. And you've heard their side of the story. Now, why don't you meet customers and listen to their side of the story?'

That made sense, and off the two went to conduct yet another market survey—this time with customers.

The first customer they met was Pallavi Aunty.

'Namaste Pallavi Aunty. How are you?' said Nikki politely.

'*Aao beti. Chai loge?*'

'Thank you, aunty. Aunty, we wanted to ask you some questions about your experience with Aaraampur Cabs.'

'Sure, beti. Go ahead'. And over large helpings of barfi, various kinds of *namkeens*, and the inevitable chai, the questioning began.

'Aunty, what's your experience with Aaraampur Cabs?'

'Great,' was the immediate answer, 'You girls have created something truly wonderful for Aaraampur'.

Somewhat perplexed—after all, Pallavi Aunty had been at the receiving end of some of the goof-ups—Nikki went on, 'A few days ago you had booked a trip and we had assigned a driver called Soorat Ram to you. The trip had been accepted by him at 10 a.m., but it started only at 11 a.m. In other words, he was an hour late. Wasn't that a problem?'

'No problem, beti,' said Pallavi Aunty with a smile. 'I grabbed the chance to have some tea.'

Nikki and Pikki looked at each other. And then Nikki continued, 'And twice you tried to book a cab in the afternoon, but were unable to, because no driver responded.'

'Yes, I remember. But that's okay. I decided to take a nap. Afternoon, you see?'

The questioning continued for a bit, but Nikki and Pikki were beginning to get the drift. Finally, they thanked Pallavi Aunty and moved on to Sharma Uncle.

'Hi Uncle. We wanted to speak to you about Aaraampur Cabs'.

'Welcome, *beta*. Do come in.'

'Uncle, you had booked a cab two days ago, but the trip started an hour after the driver, Devi Chand, accepted it.'

But Sharma Uncle wouldn't let them finish, 'Yes, I remember that very well. You see, I happen to know Devi Chand, and I called him up. He told me that he was sitting at a tea shop close to my house. In fact, he invited me to have tea with him. I had nothing better to do, so I walked across and sat down with him. Then we started chatting about this and that. And before we knew it, we had spent an hour. Very sweet fellow. And a great driver.'

'So you had no problem with the trip starting an hour late?'

'Or course not. Why should I?'

And so the interviews continued. But with every interview, Nikki and Pikki were learning something about the good citizens of Aaraampur. That evening, they had another meeting with their mentor. And a close observer would have noticed that they were visibly relaxed. Yes, trips used to get delayed. Sometimes they would not even get accepted. But the drivers were happy. And the customers were equally happy. This was not Mumbai or Delhi or Bangalore where time was crucial and people were in a mad rush to save those few precious minutes. This was Aaraampur, where time was meant to be enjoyed. A delay of one hour? What a godsend. Let's use it to chit-chat. Or have a cup of tea.

And so the story of Aaraampur cabs continued with both drivers and customers happy. But before I end, I must give you some great news. When I last visited Aaraampur, I learnt that Nikki and Pikki were raising funds.

Why? Did they need the money?

Of course not—they were managing perfectly well as it is. It's the done thing, you see? How can you be called a startup if you don't raise funds?

That's right. Forget Bangalore, Gurgaon, Chennai and all those other non-entities. Even faraway Silicon Valley in the USA. Because our sleepy little town had now well and truly arrived on the startup scene.

12

Those Wonderful Med Certs

This is another story about 'The PITS'—the famous engineering college at Aaraampur, where Kaptaan Sahib's daughter, Manju, was a proud student.

Now by a strange quirk of fate, his elder son, Sanju, was also a student over there. However, I must mention that there was a significant difference of opinion between father and son, regarding the purpose behind attending this college. Kaptaan Sahib had sent his son to college to study. Like all fathers, he wanted Sanju to get good grades and subsequently, follow it up with an MBA from a prestigious institute. After which of course, he would get a great job. And then his mother would take over and start pressurizing him to get married . . .

But let's not get swayed by family politics. Let's focus on the first step, namely his college education.

As you might imagine, Sanju did not agree with his father regarding the purpose of his stay at PITS. Unlike his sister, he was not a model student. No sir, Sanju was a *fatru*!

A fatru? What's that? Well, if you're not aware, let me tell you how students at PITS were categorized. In fact, this is how students *anywhere* are categorized from the time of Akbar the great, but I'm not talking about just any college. I'm talking about PITS.

Broadly speaking, students at PITS could be grouped into three different categories. First of all, there were the toppers—the brainy guys, who didn't study too much but always managed to clear their exams with flying colours. Then there were the *maggus*. These people were usually not as brainy as the toppers (I said usually— at times you did get mutants). But my god, could they slog? Every waking hour was spent in poring over their books, assignments, and tutorial sheets, as though there was no tomorrow. And you should have seen them in the exam hall. From the moment the question paper was distributed, they gave you the impression that there were precisely ten minutes left. Sweating profusely, breathing sporadically and writing desperately . . .

But enough about the toppers and the maggus. The people I really wanted to talk about, were the fatrus. Terrific term, isn't it? And Sanju was a proud member of this tribe. As you might imagine, fatrus did not believe in studying. They focused on far more interesting pursuits such as chess, bridge, cricket and movies. Or simply loitering around the college canteen and allied watering holes.

But what about their exams? Surely, they had to study for their exams?

Aha, my friend. You're wrong. Dead wrong. Fatrus did not study for their exams.

They went in for med certs!

You see, at some stage, fatrus also needed to clear their exams. But they were happy to postpone the agony. By the simple expedient of using medical certificates, or med certs for short. 'Why waste time giving a stupid exam when you can postpone it? Give the exam in the summer. Take a med cert.' That was their typical philosophy. And that forms the cornerstone of our story.

You see, the PITS campus boasted of a tiny little clinic with the inevitable doctor—a very pleasant young man. A fact that I can vouch for, since I have met him. He fondly remembered his own days as a fatru at medical school (yes, even I was surprised), and empathized one hundred per cent with these students. A perfunctory examination—sometimes not even that—and he was satisfied. No, no, not in the way you thought. He was smart enough to realize that these were all fake illnesses. He was simply satisfied that these students had done enough to deserve a med cert.

Sometimes though, even he was fooled. For instance, there was the famous case of Aaloo, short for Aalok. Aaloo was a pure vegetarian who had never even touched onions in his life, let alone eat them. When he wanted a med cert, all he did was carry a slice of raw onion with him to the clinic. Just before entering the doctor's chambers, he would put the onion into his mouth. And voila! He would throw up right in front of the doctor. There were, of course, no quibbles about this. This was a clear, genuine case of sickness, and the doctor immediately issued a med cert along with the mandatory prescription. Happily, Aaloo walked out with the med cert, while tearing up the prescription and dumping it into the nearby dustbin. His job was done.

Then there was Pandit, who feigned fever by the simple process of having a hot cup of tea and splashing the balance on his forehead just before walking into the clinic. And Bugsy, short for Bakshi, who had mastered the art of coughing as though his lungs were about to cave in. I could go on and on, but I'm sure you get the idea. Our fatrus had a collection of innovative methods, designed to get them their well-deserved med certs.

Anyhow, in one particular year, close to the exams, our fatrus landed up at the clinic and got their med certs as usual. So far so good. But now for the interesting part. After all these med certs had been issued, who do you think landed up at the clinic? Our young friend, Sanju, of course. But this is where the situation was different. As you are aware, Sanju was a proud fatru—no question about it. And he would have come for a fake med cert that was rightfully his, anyway. But today, Sanju was genuinely sick. He had a stomach upset and it was hurting. Perhaps it was the consequence of too many rotis the previous night. Whatever the reason, he would clutch at his stomach and rush to the toilet from time to time.

And that's how Sanju landed up at the clinic to ask for a genuine med cert, perhaps for the first time in his life. However, he had to wait, since the doctor was not around. Finally, he did come, but a close observer would have noticed that he was not his usual chirpy self. In fact, he looked decidedly unhappy. Even surly.

Anyhow, Sanju sat down in front of the doctor, clutching his stomach. The doctor did a quick examination, and said, 'No problem. Take these pills and you'll be fit and fine by tomorrow morning. You'll be able to give your exam!'

Sanju was, naturally, aghast. 'Sir, what about my medical certificate? I can't possibly give the exam in this state.'

'No, I can't give you a certificate. I've given too many medical certificates this term. Can't give any more. You'll have to give the exam,' was the terse reply.

Now you should have seen poor Sanju's reaction. Astounded is probably a mild word for it. 'But sir, I'm genuinely sick. You know I'm sick,' he blurted out, quite forgetting that in the process he was exposing all his previous faked ailments.

But the doctor was adamant for once. 'No. I've told you. I've given too many medical certificates this year. You'll be fine with these pills.' And with that, the doctor turned to face the next hopeful.

My friend, can you ever imagine such a stab in the back? And that too, by the doctor who was considered a friend. But before you curse this poor doctor with your choicest expletives, just listen to the background. After that, you can curse him as much as you want. Preferably in Punjabi, which is perhaps the most appropriate language known to mankind, for constructing family trees.

You see, as in all small towns, the grapevine in Aaraampur was phenomenally strong. And the fact that fake medical certificates were being doled out freely, was known not only within the PITS campus, but across the length and breadth of the town. Now here's the thing. Students were not the only ones who needed fake med certs. So did the employees who worked in the various shops in Aaraampur, when they wanted a day off to spend with their families. Or take their respective girlfriends out on a date. Or simply lounge around town. All these employees started landing up at PITS, just to get fake medical certificates from the doctor. For a small fee, of course—after all, the doctor had to live, didn't he? And all this was going on just fine, till one of the shop owners saw his employee watching a movie and laughing and joking with his family. Now just that morning, this particular employee had reported sick with severe diarrhoea. Along with an appropriate medical certificate. And then of course, it was all over WhatsApp, with all the other shop owners reporting similar behaviour by their employees.

But this is where our very own Kaptaan Sahib stepped in. When he got to know what was happening, he decided to take matters into his own hand. He went to meet the principal of PITS, along with some of these shopkeepers, and complained about this young doctor. The principal, in turn, called the doctor and ticked him off. Quite naturally, the doctor was worried. He realized that his job was at stake. And as he walked back to his little clinic, he had taken a decision. No more fake medical certificates, at least till things cooled down.

And that's when he saw Sanju waiting for him. Unfortunately, poor Sanju became his first victim. Yes, he was genuinely sick—any fool could see that. But in his current frame of mind, the doctor was clear. No medical certificates. Period.

So that explains the doctor's conduct. But spare a thought for poor Sanju. So often had he landed up at the doctor's doorstep with feigned illnesses and got away with the prized med cert. But this time when he was genuinely sick, he was denied what was rightfully his. And that too, for such a ridiculous reason, 'I've given too many medical certificates this term.' Anyhow, Sanju had no choice and resigned himself to the thought of a comp (compartment, in case you didn't know).

But there is just a little bit more to this story. That weekend, Sanju came home from his hostel, as usual. Over dinner, he heard his father proudly holding forth on how he had stopped a terrible malpractice in the town.

'What malpractice, Papa?' asked Sanju, while putting away yet another massive piece of chicken.

'Oh, that silly doctor on your campus was doling out fake medical certificates to people in town. Terrible practice. Fortunately, I met your principal, and he has put an end to it.'

Now at this point, you should have seen poor Sanju. He froze. Chicken suspended in mid-air around two inches from his waiting teeth, he blurted out, 'What did you say?'

Somewhat surprized, Kaptaan Sahib repeated his remark. After all, Sanju had never shown any interest in his father's activities.

Sanju couldn't believe his ears. With a horrified look on his face, he stopped chewing. Just to absorb the magnitude of the calamity that had hit him.

And then he shook his head sadly.

'My own father . . .'

13

But Med Certs Only Postpone
the Agony

And so Sanju got his comp, while the other fatrus got their med certs. However, that was not the end of the story. No way. You see, med certs only served to postpone the agony. Because after the academic year got over, and the toppers and maggus went home to relax, the fatrus still had to clear their exam. And there was one exam that they were truly scared of this time. Because this particular professor was known to be vindictive and he was sure to set a tough paper.

Yes, my friend, panic did set in. But you must remember, fatrus as a tribe are hardy. They don't give up easily. These fatrus realized that the enemy had to be defeated. And so, they began to prepare for battle. As in all colleges, our ingenious fatrus had devised several methods to defeat the enemy. One obvious and extremely popular method—practised in educational institutions from the time of Chandragupta Maurya—was the concept of a *pharra*—a small slip of paper on which you wrote down critical things such as formulae and definitions, which could be hidden in your pockets, your socks, or even inside your shirt. And then there was a variation, where you wrote down these formulae on your forearms instead of pharras. The side effect was that your gait became a bit strange—rather like that of a penguin—since you needed to ensure that the formulae did not get erased.

Of course, there were several other weapons in the typical fatru arsenal. And each fatru was in the process of deciding which specific weapon he would use, when a bombshell hit our wonderful college. Yes, a once in a generation kind of bombshell. Because suddenly, Sanju made his plans known. Our friend Sanju planned to break into the professor's office and steal the question paper.

My God! Break into the office, did you say? Wouldn't that be a police case? With a possible jail term? Sure it would, but then you've forgotten something very, very important. You see, Sanju was not planning to get caught!

When this momentous news hit the fatru community, there was stunned silence all over. But as the full import of this plan hit them, the stunned silence turned into jubilation. The fatrus realized that they would not need to go through the pain of studying any more. Because Sanju would be bringing the question paper to the hostel along with blank answer sheets. After which, a 'friendly' topper would answer the questions. All our fatrus had to do was to copy the answers, carry their answer sheets into the exam hall, and submit them. The plan was so audacious, and yet so easy. Brimming with confidence by now, the fatru gang stopped creating their pharras, and drifted to their favourite watering hole—the college canteen—to discuss this breaking news.

And now to the actual operation. Sanju needed a partner. No, no, not an accomplice. That's a terribly negative word, typically applied to criminals. And this was a truly noble venture. After all, what could be more noble than clearing your exam? Anyhow, Sanju needed a partner for this surgical strike. A partner with expertise in picking locks. And that's where Mohan entered the picture.

Now obviously you do not know who Mohan was, so I must introduce him. You see, some time ago, the Kaptaan family had locked their house and gone out but had lost the key. And they realized that they needed a lock-picker. After checking with their neighbours, they realized that Mohan, a young salesman in Kochhar Stores, was an expert plier of this trade. No, don't get me wrong. He was not a thief—he just picked locks as a hobby. Anyhow, Mohan was called over, and within minutes, the lock had been opened. But here's the thing, Sanju happened to be at home at that time, and he watched the entire process, fascinated. He realized that Mohan was a master of his trade. But that's not all. He also realized that sometime in the future, he might need Mohan's expertise. Being the smart person he was, he started pumping up Mohan's ego whenever he got a chance. Fortunately, Mohan's ego was extremely amenable to being pumped up (since no one else was doing it). As a consequence, Sanju and Mohan became fast friends. Therefore, when the occasion arose, Mohan was more than willing to help Sanju.

And so, armed with their phones (they needed a torch, didn't they?) and the appropriate tools—a compass, a mini screwdriver, and a few assorted keys—Sanju and Mohan made their way to the main college building that night and reached the professor's office. They tried the keys but none of them worked. But that's when the expert Mohan got down to business. He poked and prodded. He turned the screwdriver repeatedly. He inserted the compass into the lock and twisted it in multiple directions and at multiple angles. But the lock was stubborn and refused to open. Mohan was a master of his trade, but the lock was a worthy adversary. Every trick in the book that was thrown at the lock, was rebuffed. It was almost as if it was mocking Mohan. The battle went on and on, and the two friends started sweating—and only partly because of the heat. What if the lock didn't give in? What if Sanju had to give the exam the next day? He wasn't even prepared. The consequences were just too terrible to imagine.

Perspiring profusely by now, Mohan decided to give it all he had. It had now become a do or die moment, if you know what I mean. In desperation, he gave the compass one final thrust. And it worked. The lock could not withstand such force, and there was a loud crack. But before you start smiling at the successful operation, look at what had happened to the lock. Mohan had not unlocked it. He had broken it.

Sanju and Mohan looked at each other, aghast. This was an unexpected disaster. The professor would know that there had been a break-in, and the police would definitely be informed. Sanju would be in deep trouble. And along with him, all the fatrus who were sipping chai at the college canteen, waiting for the paper to be brought to them. And Mohan would lose his job. No, a solution would have to be found.

Anyhow, Sanju was not the kind to waste time thinking and worrying about the future. He had come to do a job, and that's what he did. He strode confidently into the professor's office, rummaged around for a bit, and found the question paper, appropriately sealed in an envelope. Picking up these papers, along with a few blank answer sheets, he and Mohan marched out, and closed the door behind them. Of course, the lock was conspicuously unlocked, but no one really expected anyone to come snooping around at that time of the night. The two rushed to their hostel and initiated phase II of the operation.

Now, this is where our script required a third actor. Enter the topper of their batch, Paddy. A great friend of Sanju's, as well as several other fatrus. In any case, Paddy was extremely helpful by nature, and would do anything for his friends. So, when Sanju and Mohan landed up at the hostel, Paddy was ready and waiting.

The next two hours belonged to Paddy, as he pored over the paper and—in his inimitable topper style—began to answer the questions. While Sanju and the other fatrus hung around in the background, looking appropriately impressed, and motivating him with the occasional chai. Finally, Paddy's job was done, and the entire paper had been answered. Obviously, the fatrus had no clue whether or not the answers were correct, but they had implicit faith in their topper. And anyway, they were in no position to check his answers.

That done, the answer sheets were doled out, and the fatrus began copying in right earnest. Now Sanju had given strict instructions that the language was to be changed—after all you couldn't have several students—sorry, fatrus—with exactly the same answer. And so, the fatrus sucked their pens, racked their brains, and figured out ways to copy Paddy's answers, and at the same time, change the language. While Paddy sat in the background and looked on. By the way, a close observer would have noticed a look of intense satisfaction on Paddy's face—the kind of satisfaction that comes from seeing a job well done.

Answers over, it was now time for Sanju and Mohan to return the question papers to the professor's room, along with the blank answer sheets left over. This was an easy job, but the last bit was tricky. Because they now had a broken lock to contend with. But remember this was Mohan—the man with expertise in locks. He tore out a small piece of cardboard from his packet of cigarettes, folded it, and deftly inserted it into the lock. And then very, very carefully, he got the lock back to its 'locked' position and waited with bated breath for the cardboard to do its job. Wonder of wonders, the lock stayed in position and both friends breathed a long sigh of relief. Their job was done.

Next morning the professor was a bit surprised to find that the lock opened more easily than it usually did, but he didn't give it much thought. Neither did he give any thought to the fact that there weren't too many answer sheets available—after all, the administration was not really known for its efficiency. And so, oblivious of the events of the previous night, he strode majestically into the exam hall. These fatrus had troubled him all semester, and this was his chance. He had set a particularly tough paper and was looking forward to most of them failing.

And what do you think happened? As you can imagine, most of them turned in a near perfect answer paper. Now, Sanju had been smart, and had laced his answer paper with several scratches and cancellations, to give the impression that he was thinking while answering the questions. Yes, the professor had no problem with his answer paper—it seemed genuine enough. But what about the others? No cancellations, no scratching out. How could these people—most of whom had relied on med certs—have managed such a perfect paper?

Of course, the professor could never figure this out. Ultimately, he gave up, assuming that these students were brainy and had studied during the summer. So that was the end of the exam.

But that was not the end of our story. When the grades were announced, all the fatrus had cleared the exam. And that night, there were celebrations galore at Red Hot, the only authorized bar at Aaraampur. With Sanju and Paddy being at the centre of it all. And the real hero, Mohan, who had acquired a bit of a halo by now.

With that, the story of this exam passed into folklore at PITS. No, it was now part of folklore in the entire town of Aaraampur.

And in case you happen to visit our sleepy town someday, just ask the waiters at the Red Hot bar about it . . .

14

The Bus Journey

What's the first thought that comes to your mind when you have to make a journey of say, and hour and a half? For instance, from Greater Kailash to Najafgarh in Delhi, or Borivali to Colaba in Mumbai, or Koramangala to the airport in Bangalore? 'Oh no, I'll be stuck in traffic again.' Or, 'I do this every day, and I'm sick of it.' Or, 'Part of the perils of living in a city.' Or even, 'Driving really gets my blood pressure up.' If these are the kinds of reactions you have, you are a very, very normal human being. Congratulations. Travel in our cities is an arduous task, at best. With honking, swerving, cursing and swearing being the most common supporting actions.

But have you ever tried taking such a journey in the hills? You haven't? Come on, I don't believe you— you must have. But if you really haven't, I'll share with you what a typical hill journey is like. Not a journey in a Mercedes. Not even a Maruti. I'll tell you a story about a typical bus journey that our very own Kaptaan Sahib made, in a Himachal Roadways bus. Sure, he had a car—a shiny new Maruti Swift. But he had never travelled in a bus in the hills, and he was curious to know what it felt like.

Our story starts off bright and early at 10 a.m. one fine morning (yes, that's bright and early for the typical paharhiya) at the Aaraampur bus stop in the heart of town. It was a journey from Aaraampur to the sprawling city of Shimla. The bus was parked bang in front of Jalebirams, the famous halwai, just in case people wanted to pack their stomachs with pooris and bhaturas before undertaking the arduous journey. The bus itself was fairly sorry looking, with dents all over and the paint peeling off. Not the best thing for the confidence of the traveller as you can imagine, but quite roadworthy. At least that's what the driver told the passengers quite happily, '*Yeh* bus *kayi baar kharaab ho chuki hai. Par fikar na karo, aapko* Shimla *pahuncha doonga.*'

Kaptaan Sahib was the first to arrive—after all, he had a reputation to live up to. The other passengers arrived one by one, along with their luggage. One chirpy-looking young man with a handlebar moustache came with a bicycle, which he promptly proceeded to load on to the roof of the bus. A farmer came along with four huge gunny bags, which were also dispatched on to the roof. The bags were probably full of onions or potatoes. You see, the paharhiya is a frugal person and he knows that if he carries them as part of his luggage in the bus, he only pays for his own ticket. Those bags would actually travel free—no cartage. Smart, wasn't it? And then there were the inevitable suitcases that looked as if they would fall off any moment. But then, even Isaac Newton was aware that his laws of gravity did not apply to the hills of India.

With all passengers in the bus, the driver took one last sip from the glass of tea he was holding, puffed one last time at his beedi, and climbed into the bus. With the conductor blowing his whistle, the driver pressed the starter knob. The engine shook mildly but nothing else happened. Frowning, he pressed it again, but the result was the same. Shaking his head, he got off and peered under the bus, with the conductor joining in, trying to figure out what had gone wrong.

But what of the passengers? Were they angry, or even frustrated? No way my friend, you obviously do not understand the psyche of the paharhiya. They all got off and peered under the bus along with the driver and conductor, as though more people looking around could spot the problem faster. It's another issue that none of them had the remotest idea of how the mechanism of a bus worked. Kaptaan Sahib was the first to comment. '*Shayad* electrical problem *hai*,' he offered. But his voice was drowned out in the cacophony of advice from all and sundry. 'Starting *mein* problem *lagti hai*,' said one grizzled old man, and the others nodded at this true bit of wisdom. 'Engine *theek nahin hai*', said another. And then a youngster piped up, 'Driver sahib, *shayad* diesel *khatam ho gaya hai*.'

As you would expect, the advice to the driver went on unabated. However, within minutes there was another player in the game. Chhotu, who worked at Jalebirams, promptly landed up with six glasses of tea, which were immediately lapped up. After all, how could anyone ever refuse tea? And of course, Chhotu was sent back to fetch more tea for the others. By the way, in case you ever decide to open a halwai's establishment or even a simple tea shop, please remember, the key success factor in your enterprise will be the location you choose. If you can pick a location close to a bus stop in the hills, well, you are in business, and I might even be willing to invest in your venture. After all, I *am* an angel investor.

Anyhow, after a round of tea and lots of activity underneath, the driver was able to start the bus. With a chorus of cheers and shouts of 'Driver sahib, *zindabaad*', the passengers got into the bus and settled into their seats. So did the driver, along with huge blobs of engine oil on his presence. And the bus was finally on its way, with an angry squealing of brakes whenever the driver dared to press them. Of course, the suspension was almost non-existent, causing the passengers to bounce up and down every time there was a bump in the road. Anyhow, the bus continued its rickety journey past Salogra, Nanaghat and then Dedh Gharat (by the way, these are important suburbs of Aaraampur, just as Gurgaon and Faridabad are suburbs of Delhi). A little beyond Dedh Gharat, the bus halted and the driver got down. Kaptaan Sahib was perplexed, as were the other passengers. There was no habitation in sight anywhere. No shops, no houses. Why had the bus stopped? But then, the mystery was cleared up by the conductor who said, '*Neeche wale gaon mein driver sahib ka ghar hai.*'

That, of course, explained everything, and the passengers settled down to wait. It didn't take the driver more than fifteen minutes to return. Armed with a little tiffin carrier, he climbed into the bus, and explained briefly, '*Ghar ka khaana*'. That was enough to satisfy the passengers. After all, the driver did have a right to 'home food'. And so, the journey continued.

The next stop was Kandaghat—a huge place by hill standards. Here, the young man with the handlebar moustache got off, and proceeded to bring down his bicycle from the roof of the bus. With a lot of cheering and advice from all and sundry, it was taken down. Unfortunately, however, it appeared to be a bit bent. Probably because of the four large bags of onions and potatoes being plonked on it. After all, the owner of these bags had zero interest in the bicycle. He was only interested in his onions and potatoes.

This was, quite understandably, a major issue. All the passengers got off to inspect the bicycle to check the extent of damage. And two broad schools of thought began to emerge. Some of the passengers felt that the bags were dumped on top of the bicycle, and therefore the owner of the bags was responsible. The others believed that the owner of the bicycle had no right to put a bicycle (of all things) on the bus, so he was responsible. You can imagine the confusion all this caused. Two clear groups— one siding with the owner of the bicycle and the other with the owner of the onions and potatoes. In the melee that followed, the two owners were forgotten as the others hotly debated the legalities of the case. Finally, it was left to Kaptaan Sahib to say said, '*Arre bhai,* cycle *toh thheek kar lo?*' At which, a young man, proudly displaying his muscles, bent down and straightened the bend in the bike. Suddenly the two warring factions had nothing to fight over. Somewhat nonplussed, they climbed back into the bus. But a close observer would have noticed that they were quite invigorated. Nothing like a good fight, you see.

And so, the journey continued, only to stop at Shoghi. A scheduled stop undoubtedly, but definitely not for the half an hour it did stop there. Because the driver promptly announced, '*Yahaan Lekh Ram ke gobhi ke pakode bahut badhiya hote hain.*' Half the bus agreed with him. The other half had never sampled this exotic delicacy and was itching to. Natural consequence? All the passengers got down again, and promptly lined up in front of Lekh Ram's tea shop with a huge sign proclaiming, 'Tea and Snakes'. Demanding their share of pakodas. Obviously with tea to follow. Finally, with their digestive juices fully satisfied, they boarded the bus, which moved on. And believe it or not, this time it actually reached Shimla—a journey of an hour and a half taking the best part of three hours.

Now if you live in a city, I can imagine your reaction. 'What a waste of time. I'll never take a Himachal Roadways bus, and just stick to my miserable BMW. Those passengers must have been terribly frustrated.'

Ha, ha. You are dead wrong my friend. You see, small towns in the hills do not have the sources of entertainment that you or I have. They do not have discos where they can let their hair down and dance till the morning—it's too much effort, and too cold anyway. They would much rather be in bed by 9.30 p.m. They do not have fancy malls where you can saunter around and buy nothing. They do not have cute cafes where you get coffee for three hundred rupees—in any case the typical paharhiya would find this a criminal waste of money. Yes sir, small towns and villages certainly do not have any of these. But they have something that you and I do not. They have time. And they have patience. Lots and lots of both. They are not running around desperately, chasing impossible deadlines. They are not fired up, trying to figure out how to get a loan and buy a Jaguar, just to wipe that silly smirk off their neighbour's face after he has bought a Mercedes. No my friend, hill folk are happy with their Maruti Altos and their two-wheelers. They are not desperately figuring out how to maximize their share from a divorce—they don't divorce. It's too much effort anyway. They are not stuck in bumper-to-bumper traffic, cursing the government, the auto industry in India and anyone else worth cursing. They do not take medicines for high blood pressure. In fact, paharhi blood pressure rarely rises. It doesn't need to. The blood just flows ever so serenely and peacefully through the blood vessels. There is no need to hurry, you see.

Yes sir, paharhiyas are happy, contented people, and they have time on their hands. And for them, this bus journey was definitely not a waste of time. It was pure entertainment. So was the break, during which the bus refused to start and they had the opportunity to have tea and chit-chat. And the fascinating diversion, where the driver got his tiffin carrier. And the exhilarating debate at Kandaghat, ending in the bicycle being set right, with no winner. And finally, the yummy pakodas at Shoghi.

And what of Kaptaan Sahib? Well, I met him shortly after this journey, and this is what he had to say, 'Yes, we took much longer than we should have. But it was fun. I wouldn't mind doing it again.' Of course, I understood perfectly. I have the same paharhi genes, you see.

Oh, I almost forgot. After all the passengers had got off, the bus had to go for a major clean-up job. Why? Silly question—the floor, obviously. It was winter, and everyone had been happily munching peanuts. And where did they throw the shells? Not outside, surely. After all, they were all extremely environment conscious. The only place left was the floor of the bus. And so, by the time the bus rolled into Shimla, there was a thick, cushiony carpet of peanut shells on the floor, making a cute, crunching sound whenever anyone walked on it.

And that, my friend, is how this delightful journey ended.

15

The Stock Market Comes
to Aaraampur

Sometime after migrating to his adopted home of Aaraampur, Kaptaan Sahib happened to go to Bangalore to stay with an old college friend, Arvind. On the way to Arvind's house from the airport, Kaptaan Sahib recalled the last time he had been there. Arvind had been staying in a small, cramped two-room apartment. And since Kaptaan Sahib was used to lots of space, his knees and Arvind's furniture had met several times. As you can imagine, in the battle that ensued, the knees had invariably lost out.

But this time, as they drove up to Arvind's house, Kaptaan Sahib was prepared. So were his knees. Strangely however, Arvind did not stop at the apartment complex. No, he stopped the car a bit earlier, at a plush villa.

'Why are you stopping here, Arvind?' asked Kaptaan Sahib.

'We've reached home. Welcome,' was the smiling reply.

And Kaptaan Sahib stared. And then stared some more. My god, what a villa it was. Two stories tall, with a large garden in front. And a private swimming pool as well. 'Arvind, this must have been expensive. How did you manage to buy this?'

'Oh, I made some money in the stock market,' was the nonchalant reply. But a close observer would have noticed that there was a smug expression on Arvind's face.

'Stock market? Can you really make that much money in the stock market?' asked a dazed Kaptaan Sahib.

'Well, you need expertise of course,' said Arvind. 'Hey, come on. You're here for a week. Let me teach you how.'

And that was that. During the next week, Arvind took Kaptaan Sahib through the innards of stock market investing. Terms such as 'bulls', 'bears', 'price to earnings ratio', 'online platforms', 'demat', 'market cap' and other such exotic expressions were thrown around ad nauseum, as Kaptaan Sahib was initiated into the fascinating world of stocks. (Dear reader, if you don't understand these terms, don't worry. Most people don't—although they claim to. In any case, my purpose here is not to teach you all about stock market investing—that's a subject for a future book. My purpose is to tell you a story about Kaptaan Sahib and his adopted town of Aaraampur).

Of course, the training worked. Gradually, Kaptaan Sahib began to understand the game. In the process, his excitement grew and grew. The week got over very quickly and it was time for him to leave, but by now he had been well and truly converted. Yes sir, he had become a devotee of Dalal Street.

Now, like his daughter Manju, Kaptaan Sahib was a dreamer as well. Therefore, during the return flight, he was not travelling in his allotted seat, 26B, in the economy class. No sir, he was in his all-leather lounge in a private jet. Fondly looking at the bar which had been stocked up with the most mature single malts that mankind could think of. And while picking up yet another glass of this exquisite liquid, the pilot (his own employee, naturally) came up to him and invited him into the cockpit. As Kaptaan Sahib was getting up, for no reason at all, the pilot poked him hard in the ribs. Kaptaan Sahib woke up with a start. It was not the pilot—it was the fat gentleman in seat 26C, who had fallen against him.

Anyhow, as I had mentioned, Kaptaan Sahib's mind was made up. Yes sir, he had become a true *bhakt* of the stock market. This was the way to go. This was the way to buy a luxury villa in Aaraampur (assuming there was at least one).

But by now, I'm sure you have got to know Kaptaan Sahib. And you are aware that he was extremely helpful. Yes, he had decided to invest in the stock market, but he was determined that others in his adopted town of Aaraampur got the same benefits. And so, he called his friends to a high-level strategic meeting at the Aaraampur club. The psychiatrist, Dr Sood was there. And in his excitement at the thought of making money, his squint was even more pronounced than ever.

Mr Bhagat, the landowner, had to be there. After all, no one else in Aaraampur had as much money to invest as this gentleman (although the colour of the money might have been an issue, given the fact that he was into real estate). Then there was Mr Kochhar, the owner of Walmart—sorry, Kochhar Stores. Along with several others, such as Mr Roop Singh, Mr Bajaj, and three Sharmajis. Many of them with their wives in tow.

And then the magical evening began. Kaptaan Sahib had very thoughtfully taken photographs of Arvind's luxury villa in Bangalore, and as he passed his phone around, the excitement reached fever pitch. 'This is the result of being in the stock market', was the thought in everyone's mind. Dr Sood began to dream of a fancy clinic that he had always wanted to set up. Mr Bhagat had already started figuring out which luxury villa he would purchase—not in Aaraampur, but in the majestic state capital, Shimla. After all, he needed to enhance his status. Mr Kochhar started planning a world tour. That's right—even though the evening had hardly begun, all these gentlemen and ladies had already started figuring out what they would do with the windfall gains they were expecting to make.

Kaptaan Sahib then explained the process of investing to the group. It was so simple, really. All you had to do was to register with an online broker and then you could start buying and selling shares. Ridiculously easy. Even a baby could do it. And these were all intelligent, sensible, adults. Gradually, the psychiatrist's clinic, the luxury villa in Shimla, and the world tour became more and more real. And our wonderful Aaraampur gentry went home that night, determined to make these events happen.

But what about the other townsfolk? They had not been part of this strategic meeting, but tell me, can you possibly keep such things a secret?

Of course not. Very soon, the grapevine in Aaraampur went into overdrive. Mangat Ram, the carpenter, began to dream of one more 'showroom'—although it wasn't clear what he would do with it, given that he was barely using his existing one. Pahalwaan ji started making plans to upgrade his hairdressing saloon, with the latest, most fancy chair available. You see, he had recently visited a dentist and had been extremely impressed with the dentist's chair. And that's what Pahalwaan ji wanted for his saloon. Not to pull out teeth—don't be silly—to pull out hair, naturally.

In fact, most adults had been converted by now. But as you are aware, grapevines have a tendency to distort facts. Not too much, mind you, just a teeny-weeny bit. And therefore, we had some cute messages floating around. 'The government is guaranteeing a plush villa to anyone who invests in the stock market'. Or 'The government is promoting tourism. And in the process, they are offering world tours to their citizens, free of charge' (why the government would want to promote tourism in other countries, was a minor issue, and was never discussed).

Now before I proceed, I must tell you something about our good citizens of Aaraampur. So far, they had only believed in one mode of financial investment, namely fixed deposits in the two banks that Aaraampur boasted of.

They were happy with their 6–7 per cent returns, thank you very much. Unfortunately, they did not realize that inflation was a bit higher at 8 per cent, so their savings were actually depleting with time. No sir, our residents of Aaraampur were a happy, contented lot. They believed that they were making money and that was it.

But all this changed after Kaptaan Sahib's fateful visit to Bangalore. Because now Aaraampur had tasted blood. They did not want the miserable interest they used to get from their fixed deposits any more. No sir, they wanted the bumper returns that the stock market promised them (yes, they believed these returns were promised). And so, they queued up in front of both banks and broke their fixed deposits. I am told that the withdrawals were so high that the banks almost fell short of cash, and both branch managers were in a state of panic. Fortunately, however, a crisis was averted, and our Aaraampurians got their money.

And then the fun started. Demat and trading accounts were opened in a frenzy (again, if you don't understand these terms, don't worry—I will probably write a book on the stock market somewhere in the future). Hot tips began floating around, with a local *paanwala* being the chief disseminator of such financial wisdom. People inside and outside tea shops stopped discussing politics and began discussing the latest wonder stock. That's right, Aaraampur had not witnessed such excitement since Nathu Lal, the popular local MLA, had won an election a couple of years ago.

However, at this stage, there is something important that I must share with you. When Arvind had educated

Kaptaan Sahib on the subject of the stock market, he had also warned him, 'Be careful in the stock market. Don't rely on rumours or 'hot tips'. Invest in good, solid companies. These companies will make you money in the long run.'

'And most important, *do not invest in penny stocks*. These are stocks of companies that are trading at very low prices—typically a few rupees. You must realize that there is a reason why these stocks are priced low. In many cases, the companies might be loss-making. Or the managements could be dubious, with the money being siphoned off. Or the future outlook of the industry could be bleak. Whatever the reason, do not invest in these companies. Inexperienced investors believe that a price of five rupees is a bargain, but remember, five rupees can easily become two, or even one in no time. Just invest in stable, solid companies, and you have a good chance of making money over time!'

This was eminently sound advice and Kaptaan Sahib had nodded his head. And, he had dutifully passed it on to his fellow Aaraampurians. But do you think these people listened to the advice? Come on, don't be silly. 'Ghotala industries is trading at Rs 5. *Just five rupees per share.* Can you imagine such a great opportunity? Even if the share price goes up to Rs 15, that's a tripling of value!'

Or, 'I've just discovered the most wonderful company—Phenku Services. Only Rs 4. It cannot possibly go down lower.'

And the advice went on . . .

Now dear reader, I have a question for you. Did these innocent citizens of Aaraampur study these companies? Were they aware of their business models? Did they know that there were several cases against each of the founders? And the fact that these companies were making heavy losses, that were only mounting with each passing month?

No sir, Aaraampur did not believe in such trivial details. Our wonderful men and women had no desire to study all this. The prices of these shares were ridiculously low and that was all they needed. Tips were shared in hushed whispers at Jalebirams. And at Mangat Ram's 'showroom'. And while waiting for a haircut at Pahalwaan ji's saloon. The opportunity was just too good to miss. And Aaraampurians were not known to miss opportunities. They had broken their fixed deposits and they invested in droves. All in penny stocks, of course.

Kaptaan Sahib—that sole voice of sanity—tried to reason with them. He explained again and again why penny stocks were a highly risky investment. But do you think anyone listened to him? Ha ha! my friend, if you think they did, you obviously don't understand human nature. By now the wave—sorry, the tsunami—was far too strong, and no miserable human being would have been able to stop it. Not even Kaptaan Sahib. And the town of Aaraampur continued to invest in penny stocks and waited for the results.

And yes, the results did come. The founder of Ghotala industries lost the criminal case he was fighting and went to jail. And the company was close to winding up. The result? The share price of Rs 5 came down to 50 paise. Phenku services was unable to withstand the latest high-tech competitors that had entered the market. And the stock price crashed from Rs 4 to a miserable rupee and 20 paise. The misery simply went on and on . . .

The poor citizens of Aaraampur were dumbstruck. They did not know what had hit them. All their dreams came crashing down—whether it was the plush villa in Shimla, the world tour, or the dentist's chair in Pahalwaan ji's saloon. But as you are aware, every story needs a villain. And in this case, it was our very own Kaptaan Sahib. The rumour started in Jalebirams, where a few of the gentry had gathered to drown their woes in drink. What drink? Tea of course—alcohol was out of the question, given the precarious state of their respective finances. 'Kaptaan Sahib has deliberately misled us.' 'He has made money while we lost ours.' 'Never again will I listen to his advice,' were some of the scathing comments shared. While the others around the table nodded their heads wisely.

And the local grapevine latched on to these statements and spread them as far as Barog, Salogra, and even the distant town of Dagshai. Obviously, no one remembered that Kaptaan Sahib had warned them against investing in penny stocks. No sir, that was conveniently forgotten. These people needed a villain and they had found one. That's right, he was the Pied Piper who had fooled them by asking them to invest in penny stocks. Why couldn't he have warned them? It was Kaptaan Sahib who was chiefly to blame for the misery that had befallen the unfortunate citizens of Aaraampur.

And with that, our Cinderella story about the cute little town of Aaraampur came to an end. Dr Sood continued to practise in his dingy clinic. Mr Bhagat gave up the idea of buying a villa in Shimla and went back to his old hobby of counting his cash. Mr Kochhar gave up the idea of a world tour and went back to his visits to Chandigarh. Pahalwaan ji continued to use the rickety chair that he had been using earlier. Yes, a chastened population of Aaraampur went back to their earlier humdrum lives.

And of course, the length of the queues in both banks trebled in size. You see, fixed deposits were back in fashion in Aaraampur—although there wasn't too much left to deposit by now.

But hang on. The story is not over yet. A few days later, Kaptaan Sahib happened to visit Delhi. And just for old times' sake, he went to his favourite café. As he was sipping his coffee, he happened to overhear people at the next table talking excitedly, 'Ghotala industries is down to 50 paise. *Just 50 paise.* Can you imagine such a golden opportunity? Don't miss it'.

As the excitement built up to a fever pitch, Kaptaan Sahib shook his head. This was not the cute little town of Aaraampur. This was the bustling capital city of the country. You would have expected things to be different here. But no. They were not. They were just the same.

And had you been around, you might have heard Kaptaan Sahib talking to himself and shaking his head sadly,

'Human nature . . .'

16

The Visit to AJIMS

Now, I must take you away from my favourite town, Aaraampur, to the bustling city of Chandigarh, just eighty-odd kilometres away. More precisely, to the Anand Jaiswal Institute of Medical Sciences, or AJIMS, located in the heart of Chandigarh. Perhaps the most revered medical institute in the country. Medical students would probably give an arm and maybe even a leg (the other leg—the body needs to remain balanced, you see) to get admission into AJIMS . . .

But hang on. This book is about Aaraampur, isn't it? But then, how does a medical college in Chandigarh fit in?

Aha. It does fit in, my friend. Because one fine summer's day, Kaptaan Sahib's younger son, Panju, attended a practical session at AJIMS. That's how it fits in.

I've already told you that Panju was a student at the Popular Public School, or PPS, the most famous school in Aaraampur. In fact, the only school in town. Now, all students at PPS studied biology as a subject. Further, as you are undoubtedly aware, subjects like biology require a lab. And the school *did* have a lab. But it wasn't too much more than a sparsely furnished room. With a skeleton grinning away in one corner—even though it had lost one arm over the years. Along with a couple of dusty microscopes, through which you could actually examine your hair. And charts of humans and mice, and a few other creatures. That's it. You couldn't do practical things like dissecting a frog, or a rat, or any of those yummy things that biology is famous for.

Enter Kaptaan Sahib. As a proud adopted son of Aaraampur, he naturally felt it was his duty to do something about this huge gap in the education being meted out to the students at PPS. Fortunately, the accounts assistant at AJIMS was a close friend of his third cousin. To cut a long story short, Kaptaan Sahib went over to Chandigarh, met this gentleman, and struck a deal. Which allowed biology students from the Popular Public School to go over to AJIMS and attend a practical session. Just to ensure that these young students were exposed to the real world, and not just the world of academics. By the way, this session at AJIMS was one more reason for the citizens of Aaraampur to be inordinately proud of their school. After all, how many schools actually sent their students to a famous medical college for practicals?

Anyhow, now that you know the context, let's move on. One fine day, Panju's class was to go to AJIMS to attend this famed session. They had no clue what they were going to do. But it would be fun anyway, far away from the dreary labs of PPS. Now I must tell you that this class boasted of some true luminaries. You have already met Panju, and you are aware that he was a sportsman, so he was fit and healthy. His best friend Raju was a fitness freak, and therefore he was just that—a fitness freak. His other best friend was Sonia (yes, you can have more than one best friend—there is no law against it, as far as I'm aware). Sonia had actually represented PPS at the Himachal girls' basketball championship, so she was, well, healthy as well. And then you had Subu, or Subhash, who was the school body builder. Extremely passionate about workouts, Subu was a regular at the only gym that Aaraampur boasted of. He had just been declared Mr PPS, and was preparing for the Mr Young Himachal contest to be held later in the year. Yes, my friend, that's how fit and strong Subu was, with six packs to boot. And pompous as well.

The other students were also fit and healthy, although not in the Mr PPS league. They were all sporty individuals, and regular football, hockey, or even the highly strenuous game of bridge had had an impact on their respective bodies. All except Parameshwaram Subrahmaniam S. Kuppuswamy—inevitably called Param. Our friend Param was a small made, weak-looking creature, with thick, thick specs that resulted from an overdose of reading with his nose in textbooks. Param was as averse to sports as the others were to attending classes. He firmly believed that he had been sent to PPS to study, and any sporting activity would only distract him from this single-minded pursuit. Consequently, he was quite sickly. Yes, Param was definitely the weakling of the class. The butt of all jokes. Never taken seriously by any of the others.

Now I must tell you something more. Aaraampur was a small town, and everyone knew everyone else. Well almost. So the townsfolk knew Panju. After all, he was the son of Kaptaan Sahib. And they also knew Subu—who wouldn't know a person with six packs? Of course, they knew the good-looking Sonia. But they also knew the weakling, Param. And he wasn't just the butt of jokes in school. Unfortunately, he was the butt of jokes in the town of Aaraampur as well.

Anyhow, having met the key characters in this particular story, it is now time to move on. Chandigarh was around eighty kilometres away, and it was a full day trip. Our friends boarded the school bus and made their way to AJIMS, singing raucously all the way. Once they reached AJIMS, they were taken to a small room that smelt of antiseptic. Quite natural, because it was a hospital anyway. There the professor—a doctor—explained what he was about to demonstrate, which was the dissection of a rat.

There was pin drop silence at this statement. This was most unexpected. The students had not known what to expect, but it was definitely not a dissection. Anyhow, having reached AJIMS, they had no choice but to go through with the process. So, they waited and watched, while the doctor took out a live rat from a cage. At this, our fit and strong Pipsites (PPS students, in case you hadn't guessed) blinked. You should have heard some of their comments. 'My God, he's actually going to cut it open.' 'I'm already feeling sick.' Or 'I knew there was something wrong with the dal last night and I wish I hadn't had five helpings.' Meanwhile the professor simply looked around and smiled. This was nothing new. In fact, he had seen it several times before. He then proceeded to the next step, which was to give a dose of chloroform to the rat, to make it unconscious. Having done this, he stepped back, smiled once again, and waited for the reaction of all these sportspeople.

And yes, he wasn't disappointed. Most of our Pipsites had to sit down. Suddenly their legs felt decidedly weak, and they simply couldn't trust themselves to stand any more. There weren't too many chairs available, and some of them had to lean against the tables in the room. This was terrible. Why couldn't they have bunked this class? Why did they have this stupid curiosity to attend a lab session at AJIMS?

However, we must not get carried away by the state of the legs of these Pipsites. Because the class had to carry on. Quietly and efficiently, the professor picked up a scalpel and made a neat cut along the body of the rat. Immediately, Mr PPS threw up on the floor. Raju, the strong sportsman Raju, fainted. Panju was looking glassy-eyed, and the four paranthas he had had that morning appeared more and more threatening. Sonia looked decidedly uncomfortable, and to the neutral observer it appeared that she was still undecided whether to faint or throw up.

Everyone else was in a similar state of disarray.

Well, not everyone. There was one person who was oblivious to the carnage in the room. Yes, you've guessed right, it was Param—the weakling of the class, the butt of all jokes, the person who only studied and never played. The very same Param was leaning interestedly over the rat, watching it being dissected. Quite understandably, the professor was delighted to see a student who was so interested in anatomy, as he skilfully proceeded to make further cuts. And at every cut, he had to answer pointed questions from Param. 'Are those the lungs? And that must be the heart in the middle. Can you show me the intestines?'

The others had given up by now. Mr PPS, Subu, who was now sitting in the middle of what had been his breakfast just a couple of hours ago. Raju, who had been revived by one of the technicians in the room. Panju, still haunted by the paranthas—why oh, why hadn't he had the sense to stop at three. Sonia who was looking as though she had repeatedly been put through a basketball hoop. And all the rest of them in varying stages of distress. No sir, they were definitely not interested in the rat, or in any of its components. They were just waiting for the nightmare to end, and to return home as fast as possible.

All except Param. For Param, it was a dream, not a nightmare. Such phenomenal learning! In fact, the class carried on for longer than scheduled, simply because Param had lots of questions and the professor was more than willing to answer them. Param even requested the professor to hand him the scalpel and experimented with a few cuts himself. Yes, Param had truly learnt something today, and he was absolutely delighted.

Finally, the nightmare came to an end, with a highly satisfied Param and a rat with innumerable cuts. And the class trooped out, looking decidedly troubled. As you might imagine, the return journey was a rather subdued affair. No singing, no dirty jokes. Everyone was quiet, except for Param, who prattled on happily about how cute the rat's heart looked. And how he had almost missed the kidneys. Back at Aaraampur, all the students went quietly to their homes. Most skipped their dinner that evening. Except for Param, of course.

Over the next few days, a close observer might have noticed that our venerable Mr PPS had lost a lot of his pomposity (I'm not really sure if that's the right word, but I'm sure you get what I mean). Raju did not roam around with his customary swagger. Panju and Sonia were thoughtful. Even the others were quieter versions of their former selves.

But the most significant change was that people in Aaraampur started looking at Param with new-found respect. Yes, Param—the weakling of Aaraampur—was no longer the butt of all jokes. In fact, he had become a bit of a hero.

Why?

I haven't the faintest idea. Do you?

17

The Election

Every five years, India holds general elections to the Lok Sabha to elect MPs and the prime minister. Every five years, each state holds elections to elect MLAs and finally a chief minister. And then there are several other elections, such as those to the Rajya Sabha. Most people are of the opinion that these are the most important elections in our country. But they are wrong. Dead wrong. Because these miserable elections are nothing compared to the real thing—the elections to the most powerful position in the Aaraampur club—the president. A position that is undoubtedly more powerful and more sought after than the office of the prime minister or any chief minister.

Don't believe me? Well, at least that's the way it seems. So, let's just focus on the Aaraampur club elections in one particular year. As in most years, there were several

hopefuls who had filed their nominations. But this was
largely to brag about the fact that they had 'stood for this
election'. No one expected them to win—least of all, their
own spouses. But amongst this riff-raff, there were two
strong candidates. First of all, there was Mr S.C. Mehta,
reverently called Mehta ji, and a close friend of Kaptaan
Sahib. And standing between him and perhaps the most
powerful position in all Himachal, was Mr T.C. Khosla.
Both these gentlemen were well known amongst the
members of the club. And so, the battle between Mehta ji
and Khosla ji was truly on.

Now, I must clarify something important. Mehta ji
and Khosla ji were good friends. They would visit each
other regularly. Often, they met at Jalebirams and shared
a happy cup of tea, along with the inevitable samosas. But
that was before the elections were announced. Yes, they
were friends, but this was politics. No—this was war, and
silly things like friendships could not be allowed to get
in the way. These two gentlemen stopped visiting each
other. Beer and pakodas at the Aarampur club became a
thing of the past. As did chai and samosas at Jalebirams.
When passing each other on the road, they would simply
nod curtly at each other. Yes, my friend, this is what
elections do to human beings. All friendships are forgotten
as the candidates become sworn enemies, at least till the
elections are over.

Anyhow, let's get back to the actual elections. You
see, each candidate had his close friends, who naturally
became campaign managers. I do not remember the name
of the campaign manager for the Khosla camp, but I do

know who the campaign manager for the Mehta camp was. That's right, it was our very own Kaptaan Sahib! And since you are reading this book and have become friends with Kaptaan Sahib, you are obviously in the Mehta camp as well.

With the campaign managers appointed, both camps got down to business. Mehta ji had his own constituency of committed voters. As did Khosla ji. These were a given, and neither camp bothered about them, except for a cursory, somewhat disinterested WhatsApp, 'Hope you are voting for Mehta ji. We are banking on your vote', or 'Please don't forget to vote for your good friend, Khosla ji'. And that was all that was required. No free blankets, no bottles of desi alcohol. No sir, these committed voters were not an issue at all. It was the ocean of undecided voters that had to be convinced, coerced and even bribed. This was wartime, and as you are aware, all is fair in love and war.

And so, the Mehta camp decided to hold a high-level meeting at Jalebirams. Duly fortified with samosas, rasgullas, and the like, the five-man crack team, consisting of Mehta ji, his campaign manager Kaptaan Sahib, and three other venerable gentlemen, began their deliberations.

The first and most important step, was to create a manifesto. After all, political parties had to have a manifesto. Therefore, Team Mehta started figuring out what they could promise the voters. After a lot of debate, they zeroed in on an idea proposed by Kaptaan Sahib. If elected, their team would create a kiddies' corner in the club, with see-saws, slides, and allied gymnastic equipment. There was a general nodding of wise heads around the table. Yes, this was a great campaign plank. And so, with a final samosa each—just to give them the energy for the gruelling campaign that was to follow—Team Mehta left Jalebirams, all set to launch the campaign for the Lok Sabha—sorry—the Aaraampur club.

But hang on. There is something else that happened that day. Towards the end of this meeting, who do you think walked into Jalebirams? Team Khosla, of course. Yes, they walked in quite jauntily, but then stopped. And stared. No, that's not quite correct—they glared at Team Mehta. With the inevitable glares in return. However, they couldn't simply walk out—that would have meant conceding defeat. Instead, they walked in and settled down in the farthest, dingiest corner of Jalebirams. Following which, the conversation at both tables continued in hushed whispers, as you might imagine.

Anyhow, both camps having decided on their campaign strategies, the respective teams swung into action. WhatsApp messages were created and sent out ad nauseum till the recipients started blocking the source. Many people were not using WhatsApp, and these people had to be met personally. Gradually, the Mehta camp started gaining ground. In any case, Mehta ji was more popular than Khosla ji, who had a bit of an attitude (yes, such things *did* happen, even in Aaraampur). But then Team Mehta got a rude shock. In the form of one voter who bluntly said, '*Bhai,* kiddies corner *ka hum kya karenge?* Khosla ji *toh* table tennis room *banaa rahe hain.*'

Now that was a jolt. Mr Mehta was frankly worried, 'What do we do now?' he whined. But he had reckoned without Kaptaan Sahib—that enormous reservoir of positivity. Within hours, Kaptaan Sahib had scheduled another strategic meeting at Jalebirams. And over the usual fare of tea and samosas, they zeroed in on a huge bonus. They decided to construct a billiards room in the club.

My God, a billiards room! Can you imagine what that would do to the standing of the club? As it is, the Aaraampur club was miles ahead of silly little places such as the Bombay Gymkhana club. This would be the icing on the cake. It was quite another issue that the finances of the Aaraampur club were known to be precarious. But that was obviously not an issue during election time. That was an issue to be tackled when the time came—which was after the elections. Once again, therefore, fuelled by the appropriate samosas, our warriors went out in search of voters.

As you can imagine, the idea of a billiards room was a phenomenal success. Each and every member of the club promised to vote for Mehta ji. And this was no empty promise—these people rightly felt that a billiards room would raise the stature of the club sky high. Gradually, Mehta ji started gaining ground once again.

But that's when they got their second rude shock. When one of their committed voters said, '*Arre bhai,* Khosla ji *toh* squash court *banaa rahe hain.*'

Now at this stage, I must digress for a bit. Because you need to understand how a billiards room and a squash court would stack up against each other. You see, there are those of us who are physical fitness freaks and would love the adrenaline-pumping thrill that you get from running around a squash court and smashing the ball. On the other hand, billiards has a certain class. In any case, the average paharhiya would probably be less keen on the vigorous sport of squash, than on the more laidback sport of billiards.

The Mehta camp thought long and hard. It was tough to figure out which way the voter would swing, and they definitely did not want to leave anything to chance. And that's how they came up with their master stroke—a tennis court. Something that was not available for miles. Yes, a tennis court would definitely seal the deal, and ensure that Mehta ji became president of the club. Once again there was the small issue of land. There was no place for a tennis court, you see? But Mehta ji's campaign managers felt that they could buy out the land from a couple of the homeowners who lived close to the club.

Finances? Come on, don't ask silly questions, my friend—this was election time!

And so, Team Mehta fanned out once again. As you can imagine, the combination of a kiddies corner, a billiards room, and a tennis court was simply too much to resist. Opinion polls showed Mehta ji with an almost unassailable lead over his rival. Team Mehta began to relax. The election was in the bag.

And then the great day arrived. The Mehta camp cast their votes with a bit of a smirk. They already knew the result. Counting was to take place in the evening—a mere formality, of course.

But come counting time, and the smirk was wiped out in a matter of minutes. To be replaced with shock. Because Team Khosla had won hands down.

Dear reader, I realize that you are also shocked. How did Mehta ji lose from such an unassailable position? The election was almost in the bag, after all. However, since you asked, here's what had happened. Two nights before election day, Team Khosla had realized that they were losing. Opinion polls were unanimous—Mehta ji would be the next president of the club.

Team Khosla needed a miracle. And the miracle came in the form of an earth-shattering suggestion from their campaign manager, 'Don't charge any membership fee. If Khosla ji is elected president, membership of the club will be free.'

The others in team Khosla were aghast. 'How will the club manage? As it is, we are short of funds.'

'Oh, we'll get sponsorships', was the nonchalant answer.

Gradually, the import of this utterly audacious suggestion began to seep in. Not since political parties had started offering free electricity for votes, had the country seen such an earth-shattering offering. 'No membership fee? The voters would simply lap it up.'

With that, Team Khosla went all out to spread the word. And the response was magical. 'No membership fee? Of course, we will vote for Khosla ji. Such a nice gentleman!' Or, 'I think Khosla ji will make a fine president. One of the best we have ever had.' Or even,

'I had always planned to vote for Khosla ji.' (The last statement, of course, came from a voter who had already flip-flopped four times).

By the way, do you think Team Mehta came to know of this masterstroke? Of course not—don't be silly. They were enjoying a quiet day with beer at Kaptaan Sahib's house. Utterly relaxed. A pre-victory celebration, you see?

And now before I end, I must answer a question that I'm sure you are simply itching to ask, 'Was this free membership implemented?'

Come on, haven't you heard of pre-election promises?

Grow up, my friend.

18

The Aaraampur Water Supply

There were several great things about our little town
of Aaraampur. It was serene and peaceful. Pollution
levels were almost non-existent. People were friendly and
helpful. In fact, I could go on and on . . .

But just to balance out these positives, it also had one
major problem—it had an acute, round-the-year shortage
of water. You see, water for the town came from a stream
called Siri. Now Siri is a tributary of the river Giri, which
in turn is a tributary of the Yamuna, so you can imagine
how small it is. And that, my friend, was the only source
of water for the inhabitants of our cosy little town.

And this is how it worked. The roof of every house had
a tank to store this precious water. With a lid, naturally,
to keep out insects and other similar creations of God.
This tank was connected to the local water supply. And

this was the key: the local municipal corporation (yes, the town was the proud possessor of such an august body) had decreed that every household would be able to get its tank filled *only once a week*. That was all. Within this, they had to manage their drinking water, cooking, their baths (if any), the washing of clothes, and anything else they might wish to do.

Now the reader—who is perhaps used to unlimited water—might imagine that this was an impossible situation, and that Aaraampurians would grab the first opportunity to leave town for a more water-rich environment. After all, bathing in luxury is one of the fundamental rights of our valued citizens. And how can you possibly have a luxurious bath till you've emptied half your tank? But that's where you are completely wrong my friend. You simply do not understand the residents of Aaraampur. They were patient, non-demanding people, quite happy with their lot, and with absolutely no desire to leave. Too bad if they couldn't have a bath every day— twice a week was fine. I am told that in the winters some of the younger residents made the supreme sacrifice of not bathing for two months at a stretch. With their respective mothers not pushing them too hard (I was one of the clean ones, and never delayed it beyond a fortnight). And everyone managed, as life carried on.

But to really understand the innards of this story, I must explain to you the process that the municipal corporation followed. They had appointed one person, popularly known as the *paaniwala*, who was assigned the responsibility of implementing the weekly rationing of water. And my God, was he strict? He would release just enough water for each tank to fill up—no more and no less. Now, you can imagine the fan-following this gentleman had. I am fairly certain that even on the day of the annual Union Budget, the finance minister of the country would not have enjoyed the kind of following that the paaniwala had. And did he bask in this glory? When he appeared on the roads of Aaraampur, there was a hush, as he strode majestically down whichever path he had chosen, followed by his *chamchas*. Yes sir, that was the value of the paaniwala of Aaraampur.

The residents of the town guarded their respective tanks jealously. No outsider was allowed to venture anywhere close to it, for fear of a couple of buckets of water being stolen. Fortunately, residents were by and large honest, and as far as I am aware no water-related FIRs were lodged with the local police station—at least during the time I lived there.

As I've already mentioned several times—and I don't want to repeat myself—everyone was able to manage in these trying circumstances. Including the Kaptaan household. Till one day some idiot left their tank uncovered. My God, what a disaster. Till today, the Kaptaan family looks back on that day with a shudder. Because an inquisitive rat, who probably wanted to explore his surroundings, happened to land up in the vicinity of the tank. Being fond of diving and swimming, he dived into the tank and swam. I'm sure he was enjoying himself, practising his breaststroke as well as the more elegant butterfly stroke. Except that at the end of his relaxing swim, he needed to come out of the 'pool'. And that was the fundamental problem. Try as he might, he simply couldn't jump out. I'm sure you don't want to hear more. Suffice it to say that the Kaptaan family discovered a very, very dead rat in the tank the next morning.

Now, you would rarely have seen Madam Kaptaan in such a frantic state. 'God, what will we do? First of all, we need lots of water to clean up the mess. And then we have the rest of the week. No water. How will we manage?

And that's when our good Kaptaan Sahib set off in search of the paaniwala. But do you think this gentleman would listen to reason? No way, my friend, he was adamant. *'Aapne* tank *khula kyon rakkha?'* was all that he would say. Finally, after a lot of coaxing and cajoling, Kaptaan Sahib resorted to that age-old tactic known to mankind. You know, the method that works every time. *'Bhai sahib, yeh leejiye. Bachhon ki mithai ke liye.'* Finally, the gentleman relented, after having carefully checked up on the quantum of 'mithai' that was being proposed, and released just enough water to wash the tank thoroughly and fill it up again. *'Dobara nahin karoonga'*, was his parting shot, as he strode away majestically.

And with that, life returned to normal. Till one day, some relatives of the Kaptaan family landed up from Delhi. Husband, wife, son and daughter. Very friendly people, but oh, so clean. The moment they landed up, the daughter announced that she was going to have a bath. Unfortunately, the Kaptaan family did not realize the implications of this momentous statement, as the young girl proceeded to clean up the remnants of the long, dusty journey from Delhi. And then the son wanted to do the same. Except that somewhere in the middle of his bath, he started shouting, '*Paani khatam ho gaya.*' And strode out, all covered with soapy lather, looking most frustrated. Cursing their folly for not having warned our guests in time, Madam Kaptaan rushed to the neighbours. Fortunately, the neighbours were extremely sweet, parting with half a bucket of the elixir, saying, '*Agli baar hum aapse lenge.*'

And so the 'paaniwala-chasing game' began all over again.' But by now Kaptaan Sahib had learnt his lesson and rather than beating around the bush, started off with '*bachhon ke liye mithai.*' Faced with an extremely attractive exchange offer of '*mithai ke liye paani*', the paaniwala agreed. But with the following parting shot, '*Bauji, aapne toh aadat bana li hai.*'

Kaptaan Sahib returned home looking quite smug with the deal he had clinched. However, as a corollary, his guests suddenly remembered an extremely important engagement that required their presence in Delhi, and had to return home. They were extremely apologetic about cutting their visit short, but of course, the Kaptaan family was equally understanding. By the way, a close observer would have noticed that the guests wrinkled up their noses when they were leaving. And I am quite sure their first port of call in Delhi would have been the swimming pool in their local club.

And so life carried on. Till one fine day, when the full-time maid of the Kaptaan family put in her papers. Well not quite. She was illiterate, and therefore could not really put in her papers, but you get the message, don't you? That's right, she announced that she was resigning from the plum position that she had hitherto occupied. Completely flustered, Madam Kaptaan reached out to all her contacts to try and get a replacement. Potential replacements did come in, but somehow, nothing worked out. And the search for that elusive maid continued . . .

One day, an unlikely-looking applicant named Malti walked up (or rather waddled up) to the Kaptaan house. Unfortunately, this particular applicant looked rather unkempt, and in fact reeked of laziness. All questions that were posed to her were answered with an extremely disinterested, *'nahin karoongi,'* or *'pata nahin'*, or simply evaded. Quite obviously, she would be a terrible worker. The family had given up on her, till they saw someone lurking around in the background. On closer inspection, it turned out to be the Aaraampur paaniwala. But here's the thing—he was not his usual arrogant self. This was a very humble, almost servile paaniwala.

'Aap yahaan kaise?' Kaptaan Sahib asked him. And the answer really hit him, *'Bauji, woh Malti meri chhoti behen hai.'*

In a flash, the family understood. Clearly, his sister was unable to get suitable employment anywhere. For obvious reasons. And this gentleman was desperate to help her out with his contacts. Quickly, the Kaptaans went into a huddle. This lady was obviously a terrible maid, but having the paaniwala's sister in the house was an offer they simply could not refuse. Therefore, by a unanimous vote, Malti was given employment in the household.

And what about the paaniwala? I can't tell you how grateful he was. Putting his hands together in a fervent 'namaste', he said, '*Bauji, kabhi bhi* problem *ho, toh mujhe yaad karna.*' And with that, he left. But not without leaving the Kaptaans in ecstasy.

After all, if a family gets two whole tanks of water a week, well, what more can they possibly ask for?

19

Our Friend Chetu

When I was writing this book, I spoke to Kaptaan Sahib several times. And on one of these occasions, he asked me, 'Have you written about Chetu?'

'Well, no,' I replied uncertainly.

'You must write about him. No book about Aaraampur can be complete without Chetu.'

And that's how Chetu appears in this book. One of the brightest, chirpiest people known to mankind, Chetu lived in a village close to Kaptaan Sahib's house in Aaraampur. His parents had named him Chet Ram, but over time his name had been shortened to a much more manageable Chetu. You see, with this shortened version, it took far less effort to address him.

Now, I am sure you would want to know how the Kaptaan family met this gentleman. You see, one fine day, the family decided that their house needed to be painted. The existing paint was peeling off, and in any case, everyone had got a little fed up with the damp, fungus-infested patches on most of the walls. And so, with the appropriate fanfare, 'project house painting' was launched.

Now, this was the first time the family had got the house painted. Naturally, they were not aware of any potential practitioners of this particular trade. The obvious thing was to ask a neighbour. 'Try Chetu,' the neighbour suggested, 'We have never tried him out, but we know he is a painter.' Since the Kaptaans did not seem to have any other options, they agreed. 'How do we contact him?' they asked. 'Don't worry,' said the helpful neighbour, 'His wife's sister's husband's friend's niece works in our house, and we will send a message through her.'

So that was that. The Kaptaans waited for Chetu's wife's sister's husband's friend's niece to convey the message. And my God, was she quick! The next morning, a smiling, not-so-young man of about sixty landed up at their doorstep and introduced himself as the one and only Chet Ram in Aaraampur. 'Painting *karaani hai sahib*?' Kaptaan Sahib replied in the affirmative and Chetu beamed. '*Main kar doonga.*' With that, he proceeded to take a tour of the house, examining the walls, doors, windows, and anything else that required a fresh coat. Having done this, he gave a quote—very reasonable even by Aaraampur standards—and the deal was clinched. Chetu was to start work the next day. With a huge, toothy grin and a namaste, he was gone.

The next morning saw our not-so-young Chetu land up at the house, armed with all the paraphernalia that painting requires. I must say he was hard-working, because he continued at the job without a break, only pausing for the occasional beedi. And this continued for another ten days, till finally the painting was done. With a touch of pride, he stepped back and surveyed his handiwork. '*Kaisa hai, bauji?*' The Kaptaans nodded, paid him, and off he went.

Now I have told you that the painting was over, but there was a vague feeling among the Kaptaans that something had gone wrong. They couldn't quite place it, but yes, something was definitely amiss. However, Chetu's optimism and confidence had rubbed off on to them and they were content with the results.

Two days later, some friends dropped in for a cup of tea. As is usual in such get-togethers, the conversation centred around the state of the Indian economy and the skyrocketing prices. Laden with oodles of advice for the prime minister, of course. And then it veered around to more specific subjects. 'So, you were planning to get your house painted', asked the guests. 'When?'

The Kaptaans looked at each other. 'But we've just got it done.'

'Oh,' was the response, as the guests looked at each other. And the silence was deafening. 'Oh, OK.' And they quickly changed the topic. Now had you been there, you would have noticed that these usually garrulous people had gone quiet. If you had been even more observant, you would have noticed them squirming in their seats, even refusing the mandatory fourth cup of tea. And they also left early, saying something about some urgent pending work (which, by the way, had never come up till then).

When they were leaving, the Kaptaans heard them whispering to each other, 'Poor guys. Someone has fooled them. Wasn't their house much less dingy and patchy before the painting?' They thought the Kaptaans hadn't heard, but of course they had. And that was it. Chetu had successfully converted a bright, happy looking house into a dingy one, complete with blotchy walls. So much so, that it was perhaps better not to have got the painting done in the first place. And that was the Kaptaan's first encounter with Chetu. A bright, extremely cheerful paharhiya, but definitely not the best at his job.

Ever since then, the family's fortunes became inexorably linked with those of Chetu. A few weeks later, they decided to take care of the window in their bedroom. You see, it just wouldn't shut. And you can imagine how cold the bedroom would become in winter—remember this was in the hills. The family started asking around for a carpenter who could do the job. Mangat Ram (remember him from our first story?) was a distinct possibility, but this appeared too small a job for such a big-time contractor. In any case, by this time Mangat Ram's 'reputation for hard work' had travelled far and wide, and the Kaptaans definitely wanted the job done before winter. So, it had to be someone else. Someone who could do the job quickly. Fortunately, their maid provided the answer, '*Aap Chetu ko kyon nahin poochhte ho?*'

'Chetu? *Woh painter*?' asked Kaptaan Madam with a shudder. That name brought back painful memories, you see. *'Woh lakdi ka bhi kaam karta hai?'*

'Haanji. Bahut achha kaam karta hai.'

For the next week, the family debated long and hard. Their earlier experience with Chetu had been quite a disaster, but no one else was willing to come over for such a small job. And so, with winter almost on their heads, they made a crucial decision. Chetu it would be. After all, what could go wrong with such a simple job? And anyway, he had got a strong and highly positive recommendation from their maid.

And that is how the toothy grin was back at the house. Armed with the appropriate tool bag. He actually looked most professional, and the doubts of the Kaptaan household were put to rest. Maybe the earlier occasion had been an exception. In any case, the Kaptaans were all positive thinkers.

And believe it or not, Chetu did a fine job. He trimmed the window so that it shut very, very smoothly. Just perfectly, in fact. There was only one small problem. He had trimmed it so much, that there was a gap between the window and the frame. About an inch in width. And when the wind blew—which happened much of the time in Aaraampur—it decided to focus on the gap. The result? The Kaptaans had a super cold bedroom and faced the prospect of a highly unpleasant winter.

Of course, this was pointed out to Chetu. But do you think he was apologetic? Come on, you obviously don't know him. With his trademark toothy grin, all he could say was, '*Bauji, thodi chhoti ho gayi. Par aap fikar na karo. Main nayi khidki banaa doonga.*'

The family blanched at the prospect of the entire window being at the mercy of Chetu. The opinion was unanimous. 'No way,' they said. And then Chetu showed them why he was such a master of *jugaad*. He asked for an old piece of cloth, stuffed it into the gap, stepped back and proudly surveyed his handiwork. '*Dekho. Bilkul theek ho gayi.*'

And he was dead right. The wind had been blocked effectively. Of course, what he had done to the aesthetics of the house is another story.

For the next several weeks, the Kaptaan family lived in dread of something going wrong in the house and requiring the expertise of Chetu. Fortunately, fate was on their side, and nothing did go wrong. One fine day, however, they had gone to a friend's house for dinner. As usual, the follies of all the prime ministers over the past twenty years were discussed threadbare. But ever so often, this discussion would pause. You see, for no apparent reason, two of the lights in the house would go on and off almost at will, without any human intervention. Most distracting, as you can guess, particularly when vital issues regarding the future of the country were being discussed.

'It's a loose connection, you see,' said their friend apologetically, after the umpteenth on-and-off cycle, and tried to brush the issue aside.

But the Kaptaans were smart. In a flash, they realized what had happened. 'Who did the wiring for these lights?' asked Kaptaan Sahib. 'Was it Chetu?'

'How did you know?' was the immediate response. But there was no need to explain. The knowing smiles of the Kaptaan family told the story.

As you can imagine, over the years, stories of Chetu's exploits with his little tool bag spread along the length and breadth of Aaraampur. No one really wanted to call him over, but in many cases, they did not have a choice. And so, Chetu happily left his mark on more and more households in Aaraampur.

And that was our friend Chetu. Extremely cheerful, but definitely not the best at his trade—and by the way, he had plenty of trades. The town of Aaraampur also discovered that in the true tradition of our erstwhile maharajas, he had two wives, who he kept in two different villages. To avoid any possible contact, you see? I am still not sure why two different women had fallen for him. Perhaps they were impressed by the plethora of skills he possessed.

Some years later, as you are aware, the Kaptaans moved out of Aaraampur and returned to Delhi. But Kaptaan Sahib had always had a soft corner for the Himachal hills and made several trips back to Aaraampur. During one of these trips, he sought Chetu out. He found Chetu in his village, an old man barely able to speak. But the toothy grin was still there—with bright pink gums replacing the teeth.

During this visit, Kaptaan Sahib also happened to meet Chetu's son, Bihari Lal. While sipping a cup of tea provided by Chetu's daughter-in-law, with the mandatory two large spoons of sugar, he asked Bihari Lal, '*Kya kaam karte ho*, Bihari Lal?'

'*Bauji, main* painting *ka kaam karta hoon. Aur lakdi ka bhi.*'

Quite intrigued, Kaptaan Sahib continued, '*Bijli ka bhi?*'

'*Haanji.*'

Beside himself with excitement by now, Kaptaan Sahib asked, '*Aur kuchh?*'

'*Bauji, jo bhi kaam mil jaaye. Maine* plumber *ka bhi kaam kiya hai.*'

'*Woh dekho ji. Woh almaari inhoney banayi hai*', piped up his wife, gazing proudly at her husband. Kaptaan Sahib looked in the direction she had pointed to and saw a sorry-looking cupboard, which reminded him vaguely of the Leaning Tower of Pisa. But being the polite person that he was, he made the appropriate appreciative noises. After all, he couldn't disappoint a devoted paharhi wife, could he?

And that was that. Chetu had retired, but his son had kept the family flag flying proud and high. Kaptaan Sahib gave a bit of money to Chetu and walked out of his house, marvelling at his second lesson in genetics.

Yes sir, Chetu had retired, but his genes were carrying on merrily. Perhaps in an amplified version . . .

20

The Wrestling Championship

And now for the crowning glory. The one event that every citizen of Aaraampur is truly proud of. You see, every four years the world wakes up to the biggest sporting event in history—the Olympics. And every year our country wakes up to something which is perhaps even bigger, and definitely noisier—the IPL. But believe me, these are trivial events compared to the real thing. The real thing, ladies and gentlemen, is neither of these. The real thing is the annual Aaraampur wrestling championship, which takes place at the picturesque Jagat Singh ground in the heart of town. Yes sir, ask any resident of Aaraampur whether he has heard of the Olympics, and he will probably nod disinterestedly, if at all. But ask anyone about the Aaraampur wrestling championship and you will see his face light up in excitement. Because this is what people wait for year after year. This is a true sporting extravaganza, beyond everything else.

People come from far and wide to participate in this championship. From exotic places like Barog, Kandaghat and Dagshai. And before I forget, even transatlantic places like Sanjauli and Narkanda. It is as if the world forgets everything else and simply lands up at Aaraampur.

There are bouts in different weight categories, all the way from a miserable 50 kg to an impressive 90+ kg. As you can imagine, the participants in lower-weight categories invite sniggers at times. *'Dekho chhotu ko,'* or, *'Kitna mariyal hai. Usko toh mai bhi haraa doonga,'* are just a sampling of the derisive comments thrown at these poor souls. But the true fascination is reserved for the heavyweight category—the crown jewel of the championship. The massively impressive 90+ kg category. This is what the audience comes to see. Those huge hulks, lumbering around with their respective paunches bobbing up and down in complete synchronism. And when the winner finally emerges, the crowd lets out a collective breath, saying, 'Hush gentlemen, a man has come to town'. Yes my friend, if you haven't seen these heavyweight bouts in the Aaraampur wrestling championship, you have missed something in your miserable life. And I would strongly urge you to add this to the other, lesser-known wonders of the world that you might have seen, such as the Taj Mahal, the Niagara Falls, the Eiffel Tower, and other such non-entities.

Now, this particular year was a bit special. Because this year Aaraampur had its very own Lachhi Ram, the reigning champion in the heavyweight category. How impressive he looked, standing tall at five feet two inches. And the mandatory paunch, which actually made him look even more distinguished, if that were possible. Yes, ladies and gentlemen, Lachhi Ram was the envy of all the menfolk in town. And strictly between you and me, several of the womenfolk would steal wistful glances at him—when their husbands were not around, of course.

Lachhi Ram's bout was to be the crowning glory of the tournament. The final, as it were. And no stone was left unturned to ensure that our reigning champion reigned once again. His opponent was known to be a capable wrestler called Kartar Singh, from far-away Jalandhar in Punjab. But that did nothing to dim the confidence of the residents of Aaraampur. They were supremely confident. Jalandhar or New York, there was no one to compare with their own Lachhi Ram. He would win hands down, that was a certainty. The only question was—how long would his opponent last? Bets were laid thick and fast—in the currency of either tea or bundles of beedis. You see, our good people of Aaraampur were definitely not mercenary. Money meant nothing to them. Sitting in the sun with a glass of tea and a beedi between finger and thumb—that was all they asked for.

There were, however, two issues. First of all, like all Olympians before him, Lachhi Ram needed a manager. A good, solid, professional manager, who would leave Lachhi free to focus on his wrestling skills. Now that wasn't difficult to find. That's right, it was our very own Kaptaan Sahib, who was by now, one of the favourite sons of Aaraampur. So that was taken care of. The other issue was that Kartar Singh was known to be a decent wrestler, perhaps with knowledge of the latest techniques. To fight against him, Lachhi Ram would need to be coached in these techniques as well. And for that, he needed a professional coach, in addition to a manager. Perhaps for the entire month before the championship. Now, where would he get such a coach? Someone with experience, who could guide him?

And that's where Kaptaan Sahib swung into action. He put on his thinking cap and thought and thought. He even toyed with the idea of bringing in a foreign coach (no, not from a foreign country—don't be silly, from the nearby town of Tattapani). When suddenly, in a fit of brilliance, he hit upon the perfect solution. Of course! The Pahalwaan Nai! Why didn't he think of him earlier? He had the experience. He had the confidence. And above all, he had the wisdom that is critical for any wrestling coach. And so, leaving his cup of tea half-finished (a sacrilege for any paharhiya), he strode across to Pahalwaan ji's saloon.

Pahalwaan ji was utterly magnanimous in his response, *'Aaraampur ke liye kuchh bhi karne ko tayyaar hoon,'* he said. And that was that. Pahalwaan ji was appointed chief coach to the reigning champion.

However, there was one issue that remained to be sorted out. Just as wrestling is a full-time occupation, so is coaching. You cannot have the coach chopping someone's hair, running to the *akharha* for a ten-minute coaching stint, and then running back again to the saloon for a shave. No, that would not do at all. But our Pahalwaan ji was magnanimous. And in any case, you are aware that to the average paharhiya, money means next to nothing. So he shut down his saloon for a full month and devoted all his time to coaching Lachhi Ram.

As you may have guessed, this utterly selfless decision did result in some collateral damage. For the next month or so, a casual visitor to Aaraampur would have noticed a quaint trend among the men of Aaraampur. They all sported long hair, hippy style. Those who did not know the background assumed this was a new style that had caught on in town. But you and I know better, don't we ☺?

Anyhow, this was a small price to pay for the larger good of the town, as the coaching continued. Every morning at the crack of dawn (11 a.m. to be precise— remember this was a hill town), Lachhi Ram, along with his manager Kaptaan Sahib, and his coach Pahalwaan ji, were seen at the Jagat Singh ground where the bouts were to be held. And right through the day, till 12 noon sharp, the coach and his pupil went through the drill, while Kaptaan Sahib watched the proceedings with a hawk's eye. Sit-ups, tea, push-ups, more tea with a few samosas, sit-ups once again, still more tea. You see, the cardinal rule of any world-class sport is that calories that are expended must be replaced.

Fortunately, they had a highly efficient manager in Kaptaan Sahib, who provided all the nourishment required. At noon all three of them were exhausted, and after a hearty meal of paranthas they snored away through the afternoon. Only to be back again bright and early the next morning, for the same punishing routine.

And you should have seen the crowds watching them train. Devoted is not the word. *'Kitni mehnat kar rahey hain teenon. Bhagwan inko saphalta dey.'*

Finally, the great day arrived. And you should have seen the crowd. Men from the surrounding villages came in freshly starched kurta pyjamas. Women came in bright saris, with huge necklaces and earrings. This was a special event, and they could not possibly be seen to be less well dressed than their neighbours. It is another issue that being well dressed appeared to mean 'loud and garish' but then who could grudge them their choice?

So that was the crowd. And then the minor bouts were gone through. But then—hold your breath—it was time for the real thing. The bout that would decide the heavyweight champion of Aaraampur for the next 365 days. There was a collective gasp from the audience as the two contestants stepped into the ring. (Ring is a symbolic term—it was actually a circular area of soft mud, which had been dug up for the purpose. But you can assume it was a ring. It makes absolutely no difference to our story). With both the coach and the manager watching from the sidelines, as though their entire future depended on this bout. As the contestants glared at each other and riled themselves up, the crowd also got into the act. Frenzied cheering broke out. Loud shouts of 'LACHHI, LACHHI,' and 'AARAAMPUR, AARAAMPUR' through the length and breadth of the ground (I am told by reliable sources that these chants were also heard in the neighbouring villages, but I suspect that is a bit of an exaggeration). Some of the more enterprising ones in the crowd were a bit more specific, *'MAAR DO SAALEY KO! PEET DO!!'* It was a three-minute bout, but the crowd wanted their hero to finish it off in style within a minute.

And then there was a kind of hush. All over the ground. As the two wrestlers—the home favourite Lachhi Ram, and the villain of the piece, Kartar Singh, closed in. You could see their skills in action as they circled each other warily, not wanting to get trapped. Suddenly Lachhi Ram lunged forward—motivated by the cheering naturally—but Kartar Singh deftly evaded his grasp. As deftly as a 90+ kg human being can. Once again Lachhi Ram made a swift move and once again Kartar Singh escaped. Again and again the frustrated Lachhi Ram attempted to attack Kartar Singh, but each time Kartar Singh evaded him. The crowd began to get restless. *'Bhaagta kyon hai? Mard ki tarah saamna kar,'* was the general chant. Trusting his animal instincts by now, Lachhi Ram moved in for the kill. But Kartar Singh was ready. He bent down, picked up Lachhi Ram by one leg, swung him around, and deposited him on the ground. The bout was over. In precisely two minutes.

There was stunned silence all around. You could have heard the silence as far away as Kandaghat. Their reigning champion defeated? In just two minutes? How could this possibly happen? Disbelief filled the air as poor Lachhi Ram got up with a grim expression and prepared to walk out.

And what of our coach and manager? They couldn't believe their eyes. All that gruelling hard work over the past month, along with the paranthas and samosas and the few buckets of tea, gone down the drain in two minutes flat? They stared at each other in stunned silence.

And what of the crowd? You might think that they would cheer for the victor. But no, they were too badly jolted. All they could think of was that their beloved Lachhi Ram, the pride of Aaraampur, had lost. To some silly outsider, from a place called Jalandhar. While Kartar Singh stood nonchalantly, as though he had known it all along.

And what do you think happened next? Did the entire crowd disperse in gloom? My friend, if that's what you think, you have not studied the paharhi mind. The average paharhiya is unabashedly positive. Suddenly, one of them had a brainwave. '*Yeh doosra* Punjab *ka* champion *hai. Aur hamare* Lachhi Ram *ne usey do mint tak rokey rakkha*' (by the way, 'mint' is the correct way to pronounce the word minute, so you'd better learn it).

That was the spark the crowd needed. 'Punjab *ka* champion? *Aur* Lachhi *do mint tak mukabla karta raha? Wah re* Lachhi!!' And the crowd roared once again, 'LACHHI, LACHHI, AARAAMPUR, AARAAMPUR.' And for good measure, 'PAHALWAAN JI, KAPTAAN SAHIB,' as well. So what if Lachhi Ram had lost? So what if the other guy was not the champion of Punjab? Someone had said so, and therefore he must have been the champion of Punjab. Paharhiyas do not lie, as you know. And what about Lachhi Ram? Well, with each chant, his chest swelled up further and further. Even he began to believe that he was the real champion—having lasted a full two minutes. And you can guess what happened next. Lachhi

Ram was promptly lifted on to the shoulders of the crowd (it took four able-bodied young men to do so) and paraded across the length and breadth of the Jagat Singh ground.

And what about Kartar Singh? No one really bothered, as he looked on, amused.

In the days to come, Lachhi Ram became even more of a hero than before—if that were possible. And our Pahalwaan ji was delighted. '*Mera chela do mint tak kushti karta gaya*,' he kept repeating ad nauseum to anyone who happened to sit in his barber's chair. While Kaptaan Sahib strutted about the town with quiet pride.

But that was not all. In his delight, our Pahalwaan ji announced that all haircuts for the next week would be free. Aaraampurians flocked to his saloon—after all, this was an even bigger offer than the annual Amazon Diwali sale. So our Pahalwaan ji snipped away happily.

And slowly, ever so slowly, our sleepy little town of Aaraampur returned to normal . . .

21

Now That You've Been There . . .

So now you have been to the sleepy little hill town of Aaraampur.

And you have met wonderful people like Kaptaan Sahib, and the Pahalwaan Nai, and Chetu, and Dr Sood, the psychiatrist. And many, many more. And you have also seen the wonderful Aaraampur club. Which would give a terrific inferiority complex to lesser-known clubs like the Bombay Gymkhana club. You have also seen PITS—one of the most respected engineering colleges in the country. And . . .

But wouldn't you *really* like to go to Aaraampur? Not just through my book, but actually take a train or a cab and land up there? And meet all those wonderful characters that you have met through this book? And see for yourself why the PITS is such a respected institution.

Or why the Aaraampur wrestling championship would put the Olympics to shame.

That's right, I knew you would.

Well, you are in luck. I go there all the time. Just get in touch with me on LinkedIn at www.linkedin.com/in/dhruvnathprof, or on email at dhruvn55@gmail.com. And we'll plan a trip together in my Thar.

And as a special treat, I'll take you to Jalebirams.

Till then, bye.

Dhruv Nath

Acknowledgements

Dear reader,

Now that you've read this book, I must share something with you. I am from the hills of Himachal and have spent several years in the quaint little town of Solan. And you've probably guessed that the book is based on life in Solan.

You are absolutely right. It *is* based in Solan, although the characters are all fictitious. And therefore, I simply have to start by thanking the town of Solan as well as all its inhabitants, for the wonderful years I spent there. After all, I wouldn't want them to sulk and refuse to talk to me the next time I visit the town, would I?

And now I must thank one of the greatest writers of our times—Ruskin Bond. As you're probably aware, Mr Bond lives in the hills of India and loves them. Even better, he writes humorous books. Therefore, I could not think of a better person to go through my book and comment on it. Thank you, sir.

By the way, this is my third book with Penguin Random House, and I must say they have been wonderful publishers (why else would I keep going back to them?). Starting with my terrific young friend, editor and chief advisor, Radhika Marwah. And of course, Yash Daiv, with whom I had a constant tug-of-war over the language—but in the end the book turned out far better than the original. And I simply must mention Vijesh Kumar, Sameer Mahale, Gunjan Ahlawat, Aishvarya Misra, Anuj Sharma, Gopal Kabta, Saleheen Momammed and Anuj Dutta, who have always been there to help. Finally, all the other 'Penguinites' whom I've never met, but who worked brilliantly behind the scenes to get my books in shape.

This is a funny book with funny characters. But the one person who has really made them come alive is my young friend Pranay Ravi, the brilliant artist. Along with the chirpy designer from Penguin Random House, Aakriti Khurana.

My wife Rajni—the only girlfriend I ever had—with whom I spent days and more days discussing the plots of these stories. And who went through each story multiple times, to ensure they became better and better. So much so, that the book should really have been co-authored by both of us!

My children, Malvika and Siddharth, deserve a special mention for putting up with a peculiar father, who gets into long spells of hibernation to write some silly books.

Along with the children who joined the family (or maybe I should call them young adults)—Niraj and Deeksha. And of course, my parents, who have encouraged me in whatever I wanted to do, ever since I was born—or more correctly, since the age of two, when I was able to communicate my thoughts somewhat coherently.

And finally of course, baby Shloka. Who keeps wondering why Nana is always on his laptop, furiously typing away. When she's a bit older, she'll read these stories—and hopefully laugh at them!

I hope I haven't missed anyone. But even if I have, I believe I have given you enough names . . .

. . . to blame, in case you don't like the book!